CONTENTS

ABROAD

FOREWORD
Is this book for you?

Maybe you want to use the knowledge and professional capital accumulated during years working for corporations to open a consulting firm and, with the acquired expertise, be the reference in your field?

Perhaps a small startup with big plans invited you to join their first team of employees. That too makes you an entrepreneur.

There is also a chance that you want to start over, leave the rat race and the *9 to 5* journey, because even if it means working more than the *9 to 5*, you will work for something you are building, with the flexibility to call the shots, set the deadlines and create something from scratch.

However, for you it is not enough to leave your job and start a business in the same place where you live.

No. You are going far away. Maybe to another state, country, or even continent.

Maybe you hate the excessive (or lack of) government in your country or you want to live in a place with different economical perspectives.

No matter your reasons, when you tell other people your ideas, they will either tell you to *plan carefully and be cautious* or tell you how *brave you are.*

Both are correct.

It takes some bravery to be an entrepreneur. Even more to be an entrepreneur far from home.

It also takes planning to make it real, and caution to survive.

However, the first – and *sine qua non* - condition to start a business far away is the sincere willingness to do so. The idea that starting a business is what you need to do, even what you **must** do.

There is a spark, the deep entrepreneurial desire allied with the impetus of a 15th-century navigator to conquer the world. To have this ember inside you is the first step.

If you are reading those lines, I bet you already have this spark.

(Or you took this book by mistake, fault of our designer for making an attractive cover).

In the next pages, I will write about the other steps for a thrilling journey, with examples from colleagues, distinguished entrepreneurs abroad, and some from my personal experience. Things like

- Which business and non-business factors to consider when planning **where** to open your business?
- How to understand, adapt, and thrive in another culture as an entrepreneur?

- How to find local allies and what to offer them in exchange for help?
- How to screen the local competitors of a completely new country, and know them better than they know themselves.

Opening a business far from where you grew up is a journey traced by many. Some rejoiced, others not much. I am here to help you be in the first group.

This is the third book on my series for expatriates.

On *Moving Out, Working Abroad and Keeping Your Sanity*, I bring you general principles to survive as an expatriate, avoid regrettable mistakes, and take serendipitous opportunities in your way. On *Budget Travelers, Digital Nomads & Expats: The Ultimate Guide*, important practical tips and tricks learned over almost a decade living abroad on three continents are in its pages for you, dear readers.

Differently from the first two publications, this book is not only for people with plans for a foreign country.

It is also for anyone living in regions significantly different from their homes. If you are a Brazilian from cosmopolitan São Paulo, starting a business in the Amazonian capital, Manaus, I wrote this book for you. If you are born and raised in New Jersey, but just started a tomato farm in South Carolina, I wrote it for you too.

I write this book for all the risk-takers, modern globetrotters, economical dynamos of our contemporary world. Fortune hunters and pioneers.

I did it for you, my fellow entrepreneur.

Levi Borba

CHAPTER 1 - WHICH BUSINESS FACTORS TO CONSIDER FOR A DESTINATION?

Or why you should not follow your desires alone.

Pursue your passion may not be always a good idea. Maybe for small stakes like choosing beer brands in the supermarket or clothes in a department store it is ok[L.1]. But let's talk about taking risks for long-term projects.

A recent article from the University of Stanford about the findings of three researchers - Paul O'Keefe, Carol Dweck, and Gregory Walton – explained that while "find your passion" is well-intended advice, it might not be good advice.

Mantras like 'find your passion' carry hidden implications.[...] They imply[L.2] that once an interest resonates, pursuing it will be easy. But, the research found that when people encounter inevitable challenges, that mindset makes it more likely people will surrender [L.3]their newfound interest. And the idea that passions are found fully formed implies that the number of interests a person has is limited. That can cause people to narrow their focus and neglect other areas."

I am not saying it is ok to start a company in a place you hate – the entire next chapter is about not choosing a location that will negatively affect your personal life. On the other side, you want a profitable business, and for this reason, there are important factors to analyze before investing.

With the progress of your business plan, additional information will appear for consideration. Some will push you to consider other locations instead of your initial target. This is normal, and it is one of the biggest advantages of making a business plan.

You never know *too much* about your market, but often, entrepreneurs know *too little*.

The business plan is the very first document I recommend you to do when venturing far away. It is here where you will analyze if your guts are right and if the business is viable. Do not be afraid to change your opinion, location, or even economic activity. At the planning phase you still invested near nothing, so to discover something wrong and fix it has a minimal cost. The same cannot is not true when your business is already running. Do a good business plan to discover quickly any incorrect assumption.

Some universal factors to consider are:

- Demand: Is it enough to generate profit? Can I create additional demand through innovation? How can my firm satisfy customers' needs?
- Offer: How heavy is the competition? Are they profitable? What are their differentials? Which competitive advantages I should

have against them?
- Government and Private Incentives: What funding lines are available? Is affordable credit easily obtainable? Are there tax-exceptions for new businesses or sectorial incentives?
- Bureaucracy – How clear are the regulatory demands? What are the risks of the legal framework delay my project?
- Infrastructure – Are the transport, telecommunications, and other infrastructure resources suitable to my business now, and for future expansions?
- Location and Distance from Major Markets

Those are universal factors because you consider and analyze them independent of where you establish a firm. Certain places have additional elements to take into account. For example, the geopolitical risks of middle-eastern countries, or safety issues in Brazil or Colombia. In further chapters, we will deep further into how to screen the specifics of each country.

The understanding of the demand (your potential customers) and offer (your competitors) is critical to entrepreneurs far from home. We devoted chapters 5 and 6 to it. A common mistake is to analyze only the successful competitors, ignoring what you may learn with examples of failure. Here we apply the concept of *Via Negativa:* to learn what you *should not do* is easier than learning exactly what you *should do*.

Government Incentives

One common mistake entrepreneurs (including me) do when planning the funding (or capital-raising) phase is to neglect government incentives for starting firms.

I made this mistake because - after saving for a few years - I had money enough to fund the launch of my project. I never checked the incentives from the local government for the tourism industry (my company was a hostel for backpackers). I did not take advantage of some favorable financing lines from the regional development bank and left cheap money on the table. Money that later could make the difference in acquiring competitive advantages. With a hostel for backpackers, this could mean stylish furniture or a well-equipped lounge.

If you do not take advantage of inexpensive credit lines from subsided banks, or sectorial tax exemptions, you will be already in a competitive disadvantage against your opponents that explored these possibilities. They will have the financial shield to do better business than you, or survive a crisis that you would not survive.

Yes, it is great that you saved enough to finance your venture, but it is even better when you have cheap credit if needed. By cheap I mean way below your business rate of return – and use it as an airbag for any eventual crisis, or future opportunities. Mega-Investors like Warren Buffett keep money ready to invest and buy excellent companies for low prices during economic turmoils.

Even if you have cash enough to start your firm, do not ignore governmental and international funding possibilities and tax exemptions. Later on, this financial backup will make your firm more robust. It will also guarantee your survival during a crisis and allow you to acquire other promising businesses and assets.

Government bureaucracy and the two first professionals you should hire

If the previous paragraph was about not neglecting government incentives, here I assure you to not ignore how the same government can complicate every step for an entrepreneurial project.

We often relate the word *bureaucracy* to multitudes of regulations and mandatory paperwork. Form-filling mania that slows down innovation and decision-making. Startups should not have this problem internally, since they are agile and verdicts are quick. New companies, however, suffer from external bureaucracy, originated in governmental offices and regulatory agencies. While big corporations have plenty of lobbyists and a massive legal department, smaller businesses do not have the same advantage.

The good news? This is not a major problem everywhere. The *Index of Economic Freedom*[1] (IEF), published every year by The Heritage Foundation, is a good measure of how bad is bureaucracy in a country. If your destination is on the top of the ranking – places like Singapore, Hong Kong, or New Zealand - government bureaucracy will not be such a major obstacle.

Born and raised in Brazil (144th place in the IFE ranking) in a family of entrepreneurs, they acquainted me early with the complications from legal barriers and volatile regulations. After moving to Poland (44th in the IFE ranking), I felt a certain relief, even though the Polish business environment is one of the most bureaucratic in Europe.

It is a common sight Brazilian branches with more lawyers and accountants than their headquarters in the USA or Europe, just to solve legal entanglements. When I left this behind and arrived in Poland, I saw how it was comparatively easier was to start an enterprise. I decided to save in legal help, not renewing the contract with my lawyer after I established the company.

It was a mistake. That the beginning is simple, does not mean there are no traps on the way. One year after starting my hospitality business, we accidentally disrespected a regulation by not filling a legal form. This resulted in a fine far higher than what we would pay before for a lawyer.

This mistake is common among entrepreneurial expats in networking events and contact circles. People ignoring regulatory particularities because the locals say it is simple. Maybe it is for them, born and used to the same regulations that later can haunt you.

When I asked Ernest W. Adams – an American game design consultant that moved to England – what was the first professional he hired after moving out, he answered:

Tax accountant. I suddenly needed to file in two different countries and my income sources were complicated.

If you are allocating years of savings - or money from people that trusted and invested in you - and moved to start a new venture, the stakes are too high to save on legal and tax assistance.

Lawyer up. A local lawyer and an accountant are two of the

first professionals any entrepreneur should seek abroad.

Infrastructure

The infrastructure analysis is often on a second plan when planning does not focus on long-term ambitions. The need to put the company to work shadows the need to visualize a time-spam of multiple years ahead, and the future bottlenecks.

Yes, long-term planning is hard, and seldom it will materialize. This leads people to think they are unnecessary. My answer to that is to quote Winston Churchill - *Plans are of little importance, but planning is essential.*

While long-term plans are not precise, they are vital to dimension your perspectives, measure your future needs, and detect beforehand any obstacle that may arise.

As an example, I use a personal story. In 2019, while planning to open my second hostel, I found a nice building to adapt and start it there. The facility had the possibility of expansion, so in less than a year, we could double the number of rooms and the size of our business, becoming one of the biggest tourist hostels in Warsaw. All went well except for one thing. With the expansion, our internet service did not have bandwidth enough to serve properly all guests, therefore we upgraded from LTE to a faster fiber-optic connection.

At this moment we discovered that this was one of the few regions in the city still without a fiber-optics network. We never checked it before because, for a smaller hostel, LTE was just enough, but with the double of the size, we needed more bandwidth. Since the provider had no plans to install fiber-optics in our region, we needed to provide two independent LTE connections, doubling our telecommunications expenses and investments in equipment.

This is just one example, but there are others more harmful, as the case of a competitor hostel whose electricity consumption in the summer was too high for the local grid. This caused frequent shortages when everyone used air-conditioners at the same time. A result from planning without considering longer (and hotter) summer peaks. Somehow, I understand them, since it is difficult to link *East Europe* and *Hot Summer Peaks* together.

Structural obstacles are difficult to remove. Therefore, when planning your business, check not only if communications and physical infrastructures are suitable for your current needs but confirm if they are enough even for the most optimistic scenario.

Location and Distance from Major Markets

In an era where remote work is a trend and outsourcing is widespread, looks archaic to point geographical distance as a problem.

However, videoconferences and calls not always are enough to conquer a client. Dr. Albert Mehrabian, from the University of California, concluded in his research that only 7% of our communication is verbal, with 38% by voice tone and 55% dependent on facial expressions and gestures.

Consequently, the possibility of a competitor having more face-to-face meetings than you can be the difference between their success and your failure.

Melving Wong, a serial entrepreneur and founder of FanXT (sold in 2016), answered me why he moved his company – focused on reselling event tickets - to Europe:

In my case, they chose my startup to open/run our business in Paris at Station F [a startup business incubator].

I applied for their Founders Program in early 2019 without hope of being selected. I was applying to some startup programs overseas because of my plan to move my startup abroad. So happened that they chose us.

I wanted to move my startup abroad because I feel would do much better overseas (US or EU) than in South Korea at that time. South Korea was too isolated from the rest of the world in the secondary ticketing industry, and the overall Asian market is relatively small - compared to the US and EU.

Besides the professional obstacles from distance and location, there is a question on the personal side: the time zone. Expatriates underestimated how few hours of difference to everyone you know complicate contact attempts. In my first book, *Moving Out, Working Abroad and Keeping Your Sanity,* I related how this is one factor collaborating for the expatriate feel of detachment. There are other relevant non-business factors to consider, and in the next chapter, I write about them.

Summary of business aspects to consider during a planning phase:

- **Demand**: *Is it enough to generate profit? How can my product satisfy customers' needs?*
- **Offer**: *How heavy is the competition? What are*

their differentials?

- **Incentives**: *Are funding lines are available? Are there any tax-exceptions?*
- **Bureaucracy**: *How long it will take to obtain all the paperwork?*
- **Infrastructure:** *Are the infrastructure resources suitable to my plan, now and in the future?*
- **Location:** *How far we are from the major markets?*

CHAPTER 2 - WHICH NON-BUSINESS FACTORS TO CONSIDER FOR A DESTINATION?

Imagine that after considering the elements from the previous chapter, you conclude that your chosen destination offers a good perspective of profitability. Now it is time to make decisions and get your hands dirty building your company, right?

Not yet, unless you plan to be a remote manager and live in a completely different location.

If this is the case, you can go straight to the next steps (and next chapter) on the path to build your company.

But if you also plan to move to the new place, there are other things to consider. We will call this group the non-business elements. The reason to consider them is that it is hard to have a successful company if you are feeling miserable, living in a place you dislike, or in an environment that goes against your values.

In my first book, *Moving Out, Working Abroad and Keeping*

Your Sanity, I dedicated one entire chapter to exemplify why understanding your own life project is important to succeed as an expatriate. This applies if you are a big-corporation employee, a foreign student, a person moving with your spouse, or an entrepreneur.

Environmental Dissonance

A phenomenon commonly affecting expatriates is what I call *environmental dissonance.* It happens when your values conflict with the place surrounding you. In my before-mentioned book (*Moving Out*) I recounted the story of Breno, a colleague I met while living in the Middle East. Even having a good job and working in his field of specialization, he left months after arriving because the *environmental dissonance* became overwhelming to him.

Just imagine how more complicated is to suffer this dissonance while you hire and motivate a team, establish goals, write a business plan, pitch for seed capital, and so on. For this reason, becomes essential to assert that your target country, already approved in the analysis of chapter one, also matches your life project and goals.

Just be aware that I am in no point advocating you should "follow your heart" or "listen to your feelings". As I mentioned in chapter one, this is often poor advice. What I propose, instead, is a rationalization of what your new country offers and how it matches your personal needs. To this end, I recommend analyzing the following **non-business elements**.

Cultural Distance

Probably the greatest modern researcher in comparative cultural aspects was Geert Hofstede. Starting in the 80s with his book *Culture's Consequences*[2], he developed an extensive bibliography in the area, culminating with the institute that carries his name.

Present in 60 countries, the *Hosfted Insights* institute developed a model breaking down the cultural distance into 6 major areas. Below, each one of them, with the definitions from the *Hofstede-Insights* researchers[3]:

- Power Distance - *This dimension [...] expresses the attitude of the culture towards inequalities amongst us. Power Distance is the extent to which the less powerful members of institutions and organizations within a country expect and accept that power distribution is unequal.*

- Individualism - *The fundamental issue addressed by this dimension is the degree of interdependence a society maintains among its members. It is whether people's self-image translates to terms of "I", or "We". In Individualist societies people look after themselves and their direct family only. In Collectivist societies, people belong to 'in groups' that take care of them in exchange for loyalty.*

- Masculinity – *A high score (Masculine) on this dimension shows competition, achievement, and success will drive the society, with success being defined by the winner / best in field – a value system that starts in school and continues throughout organizational life. A low score (Feminine) on the dimension means that the dominant values in society are caring for others and quality of life. A Feminine society is one where quality of life is the sign of success, and standing out from the crowd is not admirable. The fundamental issue here is what motivates people, wanting to be the best (Masculine) or liking what you do (Feminine).*

- Uncertainty Avoidance - *It is how a society deals with the fact that we can never know the future: should we try to control the future or just let it happen? This ambiguity brings with it anxiety and different cultures have learned to deal with this anxiety in different ways. The score on Uncertainty Avoidance reflects the extent to which the members of a culture feel threatened by ambiguous or unknown situations and create institutions to avoid risk.*

- Long Term Orientation - *This dimension describes how every society has to maintain some links with its own past while dealing with the challenges of the present and future. Societies prioritize these two existential goals differ-*

ently. Normative societies. which score low on this dimension, for example, prefer to maintain time-honored traditions and norms while viewing societal change with suspicion. Societies scoring high here, on the other side, take a more pragmatic approach: they encourage efforts in modern education as a way to prepare for the future.

- Indulgence - *The Hofstede-Insights define this dimension as the extent to which people try to control their desires and impulses, based on the way they were raised. Relatively weak control is called "Indulgence" and relatively strong control is called "Restraint". Cultures therefore are grouped as Indulgent or Restrained.*

When I had my first contact with the research of Dr. Hofstede, my immediate action was to check how the countries I lived before (Brazil, Chile, Qatar, and Poland) scored in each ranking. The comparative results from each one - got from a tool available on his institute website - reflected with Swiss-precision the reality I witnessed living in each of them.

For example, according to the results, the *Power Distance* in Qatar is very high. This matches my observations of a place where the people take as natural the near immutable social differences. Similarly, the higher levels of indulgence and femininity (as per Hofstede's definition of femininity) in Chile are noticeable in their capital. Finally, the results from Poland fused two of my biggest impressions from living in this country: it is a non-indulgent society, with a considerable level of risk-aversion.

The two characteristics mentioned above - frugality and risk-aversion - of the Polish people contrasted with my cultural baggage.

As a Brazilian, I grow up seeing people spend a fair share of their income in branded shoes, new cars (paid in installments distributed across years), and eating out. Even though nowadays Poland has a similar income to my native São Paulo, someone will rarely buy a new car, and a 10-year-old vehicle is still OK. Personal anecdote: my wife considers it absurd that someone would spend over 5 times his salary in a new automobile. In contrast, in Brazil it is not rare to see people buying cars with the price tag of their annual salary.

This difference, summarized in the *Indulgence* factor of Dr. Hofstede research, probably affects not only me but thousands of other expatriates that move between Latin America and Europe. Sean Lana, an expatriate living in Germany, lists how other factors of Hofstede research (*Individualism*) impact his daily life.

Germany is not a country you want to be if your only major goal in life is to own a Bugatti, Ferrari, Tesla and shows off! Collectivism means the country is trying to redistribute wealth equally, at least in order to mitigate poverty and support low-income earners. Expect high taxes and you will enjoy a high quality of life with infrastructures. So if you are very individualistic, you might want to consider the next flight to another country. German organisation system is based on the ideology of Max Weber (bureaucracy), Americans practice Scientific management (Taylorism). If you are not used to obeying rigorous rules, regulations, huge laws, paper works, transparency, slow process, appointments, etc then you shouldn't stay in Germany.

It is essential to remind that cultural discrepancies - of the types studied by Dr. Hofstede and perceived in the two examples above - ***can exist even inside the same country***.

Henry Eshleman, a Park Ranger at Fairbanks North Star Borough in Alaska, USA, explained how he felt closer to foreign students than locals while in Indiana, Midwest of the same country.

In Indiana, being from Alaska made me an exotic curiosity. People would ask me questions I never got in Europe, Canada, or Mexico- "What are you doing here?" "Is it cold there?" "What it's like when it's light all the time?" And so forth. As a student, I rapidly realized I had more in common with the foreign exchange students, or with my buddy Angel, from Puerto Rico, than I did with the "regular" kids.

My biggest culture shock was essentially domestic in nature, the result of coming from a state which isn't directly connected to the rest right into the Midwest Heartland.

Even in a country with the size of a single American state, cultural differences are noticeable. In Poland, the northern region of Gdansk has considerable differences to the *Subcarpathian* cities in the south. Differences shaped during centuries of partitions between Russia, Austria and Germany. Nowadays, the differences reflect electoral results, practices and consumer behaviors.

Besides cultural characteristics, there are other non-business aspects to consider when where to start (or move) your company.

- Future family prospects: It is easy to make a decision when it concerns only you. The same is not true when it involves wife and kids. Even if you are single, it is important to reflect on what you want for the next years. If you are planning to build a family, consider this beforehand. This was my case when I decided to move out of Qatar (my previous country). My first thought was to move to Panamá with my then-fiancée, but we had plans to marry and maybe have kids in the next few years. For this reason, we live in Poland, closer to her family.
- The Time zone. I already mentioned how different time zones can create business problems. This also applies to your private life. A person in South Africa, even though is distant from his relatives in Europe, is still inside a similar time zone, but not someone living in the Middle East and with a family in South-America. This was my case years ago. The 5 to 6 hours' difference restricted the chances I had to keep contact. During my mornings, they were sleeping. During their evenings, I was sleeping.
- How friendly the country is to your lifestyle. For example, if you enjoy practicing outdoor sports, places like Dubai or Doha may not be a good idea, since it is excruciatingly hot for more than half of the year.

To go deeper into this subject, my first book, *Moving Out, Working Abroad and Keeping Your Sanity*, has plenty of considerations to reflect on the personal side of expatriation. Still, if there is one positive advice in business and personal life, it is to immerse yourself in the local culture from the beginning. How to do it is a question for the next chapter.

Summary of the non-business elements that an expatriate entrepreneur should consider before moving:

- *Cultural discrepancies*: How you will adapt to different degrees of Individualism, Power Distance, Risk-Aversion, indulgence and so on?
- *Future personal prospects*: Are you planning to marry, build a family, or remain single? How the local offer of schools, nurseries, etc., fit your plans?
- *The time zone difference*: Is the time difference considerable? How will that affect your relationships back home?
- *How friendly the country is to your lifestyle*: Of your routine and favorite activities, what you can keep or adapt to your new destination?

CHAPTER 3 - HOW AN ENTREPRENEUR THRIVE IN ANOTHER CULTURE?

Or: Ask Questions. Write a Business Plan

Level your expectations

The country I was born is one of the least friendly places for business on the planet. One reason is the humongous bureaucracy. So when I moved to Poland, I was very optimistic about not facing the same problems that my family – mostly entrepreneurs – had in Brazil dealing with paperwork.

I was wrong. My high expectations lead to the first defeats in my entrepreneurial journey, including a fine for not signing a permit request. Poland is not as bureaucratic as Brazil, but still demands a lot of form-filling and permits for most businesses.

This story is just one example of many among entrepreneurs venturing outside of their homeland. Do not take me wrong. Optimism is not bad. If you were purely pessimistic, you would not leave your country. You would not even be an entrepreneur.

Nevertheless, unrealistically high expectations are a cradle of disappointment.

Be Wide. Be Open

A common denominator marking the failure of many expat enterprises is the posture that I call *the nostalgic denial.* You identify this mood by sayings similar to this:

Oh, I cannot believe that here things go like that. This would never happen in my country!

Admittedly, all of us voiced a similar phrase at some point. This is natural. In my case, I told the same expression when I realized that neighbors, in Poland, may veto new businesses opening in their neighborhoods. You need to ask if they have any objection before you settle your company.

Even coming from a very bureaucratic country like Brazil, I never heard about such procedure, so it was my time to say *this would never happen in my country.* However, many good things that happened in Poland would not happen in Brazil too. Things like the peace of walking around without the fear of criminals.

It is not a problem to have this reaction sporadically, but to be in a frequent state of *nostalgic denial* is the formula to frustration and to harm your initiative.

If you are shipwrecked in a desert island, it will not help to cry in sorrow for not having a handsaw to build a ship. Work with the tools (and conditions) you have available.

Knowledge of cultural aspects can uncover profitable opportunities. Ignore them and your business may be dead before starting.

A first step to understand the cultural characteristics and the conditions you have on hand is the PEST analysis.

PEST(EL)

> *Hope for the best and prepare for the worst*

> *The Tragedie of Gorbuduc,* Thomas Norton and Thomas Sackville, 1561

If you studied marketing or a related field during university, maybe you are familiar with the PEST analysis. Often neglected by professionals and already-existing business, the PEST analysis is central in the planning phase of a new project, or revamping an existing initiative.

It is a model created to analyze and understand macro, external, and uncontrollable factors. Factors with a considerable impact in both the strategic planning, its execution, and future performance.

While doing my plan, I did the PEST analysis using the models learned during my studies in Brazil. It was helpful, but still flawed. The defect was that the traditional models of the PEST do not include legal and environmental aspects. Legal aspects that later caused my business to drift away from our initial plans.

In the most recent years, the reviews of the PEST added the sub-analysis of environment and legal conditions, becoming a model now called PESTEL. (If I knew it earlier...)

Instead of listing the definition of each letter in the acronym *PESTEL*, as any other business book does, here I will approach it differently: by questioning.

Below are questions you should ask during your planning phase, to understand each element. It is also possible to make other questions, adapted to your reality. To avoid surprises like the one I had, this is a good start.

- **Political**:
  - What are the political risks associated with the place?
  - What are the risks of war, revolution, *coup d'état*, elections being canceled or overturned?
  - How the main political actors view your industry? How the government approaches new or existing initiatives?

- **Economic**:
  - How stable is the economy?
  - How volatile are the exchange and interest rates?
  - Are there hedge tools available to protect yourself against drastic variations in exchange and interest rates?
  - Is the purchasing power of the local market enough to acquire your product?
  - Is the purchasing power of most people decreasing or increasing?
  - How easily can the company and

its consumers get credit?
- How are the unemployment rates?
- How easy is to hire the required staff?

- **Social**:
  - What are the cultural norms? How those norms affect the product (selling mini-skirts in Saudi Arabia probably is not a good idea).
  - How is the demographic pyramid (age and sex distribution) of the population? How is it changing in the last years?
  - How big are the differences between generations?
  - Are there any social paradigms or taboos that can affect the business?
  - Which lifestyle changes are happening?

- **Technology**:
  - What are the tech infrastructure constraints of the local (eg: limited bandwidth)?
  - Are there any governmental restrictions? Eg: higher taxation of needed components or import embargoes.
  - Is any new technology being implemented that can be a potential threat or opportunity?

- What are the regulations regarding technological innovations and access to it?
- What is the level of the local Research & Innovation agents?

- **Environment**:
  - How the environment supports your business proposition? Eg: If your idea is to sell house heaters in Rio de Janeiro, the environment plays against you.
  - How stable is the climate and how disruptive for the business can be the weather?
  - How far are you, geographically, from your main stakeholders (people or companies related to your enterprise)?
  - How people's attitudes towards the environment may affect your business model?

- **Legal**:
  - How the labor laws can affect the relationship with company staff?
  - How consumer law can affect relations with clients?
  - How Import/Export laws can affect supply lines and sales abroad?
  - How to respect both the substantive law (the actual rules and regulations) and the procedural law (the process, timing and access to

law enforcement). In some places, the procedural law essentially makes the substantive law meaningless.

Ask Questions, both from broad and specific matters.

After listing above over two dozens questions to make during the PESTEL analysis, it may sound exaggerated to think about more interrogations.

It is not. First, add your particular questions to the PESTEL analysis. Later, and as much as possible, try to answer them. In this way, you will have a near-comprehensive outlook about the uncontrollable factors affecting your business plan.

Next, ask yourself about more detailed, *micro-*oriented, questions. Elements that can be under control and even become opportunities.

Questions like:

- What are the procedures for a business visa? Do you need a working permit?
- Are there any minimum – or recommended – capital to invest required by authorities?
- Can you be the single shareholder or - like in some Arab Gulf countries - you need to have a local partner?
- What are the export/import licenses required for your business?
- What are the safety certificates necessary for your activity?
- What are the particular technical skills required from your future employees?
- Do you have local access to all the raw ma-

terial you need - in case of manufacturing activity – or you will need to import it?
- How are your neighbors and the local population reacting to the idea of your business? Are they hostile, indifferent, or friendly?

The Business Plan Phase

This chapter started with a question: *How an entrepreneur thrive in another culture?*

By now, we know that the first phase is to ask and answer questions both from macro (uncontrollable) and from micro (controllable) variables. After doing this, you organize the information and systematize the gained knowledge.

The best way to accomplish this systematization is by writing a business plan.

In some countries – like where I live - to write a business plan (BP) is an official requirement for a business visa. A BP is also helpful in obtaining credit or raising capital.

Even if this is not your case, a BP is still valuable. The venture capitalist Eugene Kleiner - an early investor in companies like Google, Amazon, and Electronic Arts - once stated that writing a plan forces you into disciplined thinking[4].

When I wrote the business plan for my first business, I gained expertise about my market seasonality and the year-round fluctuations of revenue and expenditures. This led to the conclusion that I should have a considerable financial reserve for November onwards, to not be lacking funds during winter, when expenditures with heating are very high and income is at the lowest.

While the fable of *The Ant and the Grasshopper* teach the same thing, this and other important insights for entrepreneurs come to the surface by writing a wide-ranging plan.

It took me some time and few iterations until I could write a good BP, which was useful not only to get my visa but also to raise capital on a later stage. Nowadays, for entrepreneurs in Europe and South-America, my consulting firm (*Colligere Expat Consultancy – www.expatriateconsultancy.com*) offers assistance with writing a comprehensive business plan.

The structure and chapters of a BP are usually similar between different industries. Below I list the general frame using as an example a business in the tourism sector, like mine. Feel free to adapt it.

1. Statement of Purpose – *Here you describe what is the purpose of your plan: to fulfill a requirement from public authorities? To raise capital? For your future team?*

2. The Business
   a. Description of the Business – *What are the economic activities, characteristics, streams of income, etc.*
   b. Industry Background of the local/regional market. – *An analysis of the local figures, like the number of visitors in a certain city or country if your business focus on tourism, or the number of certain transactions in the region if your business is payment-related.*
   c. Trends in the industry – *Is the industry growing? What are the recent innovations and forecasts for the years to come?*
   d. Market and competitive analysis – *Analysis of your competitors. We will talk more*

about it later.

  e. Competitor's strengths and weaknesses. – *Here you list the major competitors and analyze their particularities.*

  f. Your company's strengths and weaknesses.

  g. Government safety requirements and regulations – *Often neglected, the government requests can be a no-go for future business or collapse an existing one.*

3. Operational, HR, and Sales plan
   a. The location and facilities
   b. Staff required, salaries, and incentives – *In further chapters, we go deeper into incentives and talent sourcing as a foreign entrepreneur.*
   c. Sales distribution – *Your market channels and network of distribution.*
   d. Pricing – *Your pricing policies and strategies.*
   e. Pre-Opening Plan

4. Financial Data
   a. Main shareholders and Source of Capital
   b. Equipment and services to purchase
   c. Initial Balance Sheet
   d. Short-term Profit and Loss projections – First 12 months, month-by-month
   e. Medium-term Profit and Loss projections – second, third and fourth years, split by quarters.
   f. Assumptions that base your projections

If you ever read the book-series *Incerto*, from Nassim Taleb, there is a chance you are skeptical of multi-year forecasts. Often they deviate drastically from reality. However, the act of forecasting the next four years is not to hit the numbers. What matters is the detailed exploration of choices and contingencies.

When you take time to put on paper and calculate different scenarios, you have a clearer vision about how robust your business is to financial shocks. You establish measures to critical but possible scenarios.

Dwight D. Eisenhower, former President of the United States and World War II commander, said in a 1957[5] speech:

Plans are worthless, but planning is everything.

CHAPTER 4 – GET LOCAL ALLIES

Or: The dangers of lone wolves.

Local allies: decisive for more than 2000 years.

Gaius Julius Caesar is one of the most brilliant military commanders in history. The conqueror of Gaul.

Gaul is the region currently comprising France, Luxembourg, Belgium, most of Switzerland, and parts of Italy, Germany and the Netherlands. In 58 BC, Caesar launched a campaign to conquer the entire area, and succeeded in only 8 years. It was the largest territorial annexation of Rome so far and is until now one of the biggest military achievements in history.

Yet there was an important diplomatic component in the achievements of Caesar.

A plethora of tribes inhabited Gaul. Some with expansionist purposes, others peaceful and focused on agricultural activities. A group of tribes united themselves and formed the *Helvetii*, a confederacy based on what is nowadays Switzerland. They turned out to be one of the first enemies of Rome.

The military genius of Caesar, the state-of-art roman tactics, and the legionnaire discipline could not be enough if it was not for the local allies. Allies like the tribes of the Ambarri and Allobroges, enemies of the Helvetii. During the war of Gaul, Gallic tribes allied to Rome had important tactical roles that helped the empire to expand its territory.

The Ambarri informed the Romans that the Helvetii were marching through their lands, so the enemy not surprised them. The Allobroges marched together with the army of Julius Caesar to fight against other Gallic tribes and the Roman general described them as men of *outstanding courage*[6].

Helpful during peaceful times and conspiracies.

The same Gallic tribe of the Allobroges had a curious role in another episode that proved the importance of alliances even during peaceful times. During the plot known as *Catilinarian Conspiracy*, roman elites tried to bribe non-Romans living in the empire to create civil unrest against the government of Consul Cicero – the famous orator.

The conspirators made the mistake of attempting to recruit the Allobroges, which informed the consul Cicero. Cicero instructed the Gallic allies to get tangible proof of the conspiracy. So the Allobroges encouraged the conspirators to send them letters explaining the plot. The letters ended in the hands of Cicero, who read them before the Senate the following day, in the third of his *Catiline Orations*. With the plot exposed, the government rounded and executed the ringleaders.

Why someone would ally with you?

You don't need to be a legendary Roman general to have local allies. In a research published in the journal *Frontiers in Be-*

havioral Neuroscience, Nichola J. Raihani and Redouan Bshary investigated why humans might help strangers[7]. After a series of tests and simulations, part of their conclusion I quote below:

Furthermore, [...] in real-life individuals can choose to pursue productive relationships and abandon unproductive partners. This possibility for partner choice might select for helping behavior even with unknown strangers. [...]Finally, as soon as interactions involve multiple decisions, stable cooperation may be achieved even between strangers without any future perspective.

The research concludes that humans might choose collaboration partners according to the expected productivity of the relation, but also includes the possibility of one-sided cooperation. One-sided here means people that help you while expecting nothing back. When I asked Raul Castro, a software expert graduated in Buenos Aires and now living in Germany, if someone helped him during his expatriation, he answered:

I got a lot of help from neighbors, and people I didn't know, and never saw again.

The research from Raihani and Bshary, the example of Raul Castro, and plenty of other evidence shows that humans are often inclined to help strangers. Sometimes with no interest in mind, other times with an idea of favor exchange, and in other situations just to pave the road to future cooperation – what people call *networking.*

Multinational corporations long ago discovered the importance of local alliances and used this leverage for their benefit. One example is how Cisco, an American technology company, expanded its operations in Japan by collaborating with the local giant Fujitsu. As Rashan Dixon wrote for the portal *Entrepreneur Europe[8]*:

Partnering with organizations that are already familiar with the region can help you cut through red tape faster and navigate the business landscape. Think of these partners as mapmakers. Because these organizations have been there before you and found success, they can help you find a clear path forward.

Back in 2009, Cisco announced an expansion of its partnership with Japanese company Fujitsu as part of an effort to bring unified communications to the country. Pairing Cisco's track record of technology development with Fujitsu's knowledge of products and local business helped both to collaborate easily and bring swift change to the Japanese communications market.

The advantages of domestic alliances are not exclusive to *big corps*. Startups and smaller companies can get multiple advantages by associating with local organizations. The benefits vary across markets and industries, but here I list some of them:

- Knowledge about local customer behavior
- Alerts about government regulations and bureaucracy.
- Insights regarding market practices
- Clarity if the deadlines to implement and run your business are realistic.
- Recommendations of suppliers and services.

When I started my business in Warsaw, I had the privilege to have a beer with one of the most successful entrepreneurs in the local budget accommodation industry. His name was Hubert. We were not competitors since his business was in another region. In reality, I would be very careful in allying with direct competition, since it may be illegal. I will talk more about it later.

During our conversation, I realized that my deadlines were tight, and would be better to prepare contingency plans if things did not go as fast as expected. He also presented to me the management system that we still use to run the company and gave me a plethora of valuable advice during the near 90 minutes we drank together.

Later on, when he was short of staff, I recommended to him one former member of our team that just moved to his region. Mutual benefits, catalyzed by serendipity.

Where to find local partners – Social Media and Supply Chain.

I found Hubert, the local that gave me valuable advice, before I start my business abroad, in a social media group. Nowadays social media give us plenty of opportunities to find pairs in our industry and exchange ideas. Facebook Groups and LinkedIn connections are good for this purpose. There you can discover workshops, market possibilities, qualified staff and even ask for answers in groups of experienced players in your field. Just remember also to contribute to the group. Nobody likes leeches.

Because of social media popularity, there is a new type of ally: the local *digital influencer,* as an article from the Harvard Business Review explained:

These people are local thought leaders on social media with loyal followings of online fans. They spend their days developing new content — videos, photos, blog posts, and podcasts — and engaging their followers. [...] Their audience turns to them for industry insights, new product information, and recommendations.

They already have the trust of thousands, if not millions, of your target customers. So why not weave your brand into their story, rather than telling yours from scratch?

Digital Influencers can be a quick (and affordable) way to introduce your brand to certain market segments, like newer generations or tech-savvy adults.

Virtual allies, however, are not a substitute for local partners, serving different purposes. Remember the research from Dr. Mehrabian, mentioned in the first chapter: 93% of our communication is by facial and body gestures or tone of voice. You will not have this two-way interaction via social media posts, something only possible via face-to-face meetings.

Another way to find local partners is in your supply chain. Your providers can give you valuable advice, and since you are their customer, it is unlikely they will refuse to help. Using my hostel business as an example - adapt it to your activity – I write below how suppliers can help to better understand the environment and competition.

- The marketing agency responsible for the SEO or our website: they can help us understand where our demand comes from using their expertise in online marketing.
- The laundry provider – With their experience in serving other hotels, they know about seasonality and touristic flows across the year: when they have more laundry to do, it means that the region has more tourists,

and vice-versa.

- The shuttle-service we hired to pick customers to and from the airport – They provide us with valuable knowledge about the time when most guests check-in and check-out. Later on, this information is useful to dimension the staff needed for peak hours.
- Our system provider – The training sessions about their analytics & reporting module taught us which indicators we should pay attention to track demand and adjust our pricing.

As said before, it is easier to find allies among your supply chain, since you are (or will be) their customer. However, what to offer in exchange when your potential ally is, for example, someone with no ties to you? The answer to that comes in the rest of this chapter.

Be careful with anti-trust laws and deceivers

While looking for allies, there are two mistakes you should avoid.

First: do not break any law or part of the legal framework. Since 1890 - through the *Sherman Antitrust Act* – the United States prohibits anticompetitive agreements or unilateral conducts that attempt to monopolize the market. With such a broad definition, I strongly recommend that any agreement with allies – especially with possible competitors – pass through the appraisal of a lawyer.

In other parts of the World, like Europe, you have similar broadly defined legislation. According to article 101 of the

Treaty of Rome, valid in the European Union, even informal, *gentlemen's agreements* or mutual conclusions about pricing can be configured as a *cartel*, resulting in penalties. The reason so many conference presentations finish with phrases like *Please do not discuss pricing or enquire about pricing* is to avoid any accusation of collusion.

To explain the second mistake to avoid, let's go back to the initial example of the Roman Empire.

As much as the Romans mastered the use of local chieftains as allies for expansion, they once committed a mistake, resulting in one of their worst defeats. Sixty years after conquering Gaul, the empire made a bold movement to invade *Magna Germania,* the region at the east of the river Rhine. Leading the Roman legions was the general Publius Quinctilius Varus. The Romans had at their disposal 3 legions, 6 auxiliary cohorts and 3 cavalry squadrons, but the secret weapon was the help of local Germanic deserters, which joined the legions of Varus years before. The most famous deserter was Arminius.

The father of Arminius was a Germanic tribe leader, and he sent his young son to Rome to confirm his loyalty. In Rome, the boy received a military education, joined the army, became a trusted advisor of general Varus and accompanied him in the invasion of *Magna Germania.* Secretly, however, he escaped the roman encampment to meet with German tribes, united them under his command and later led the Romans to an ambush. All three legions were annihilated, and Varus died on the battlefield. The emperor Octavius Augustus, after hearing the news, in despair hit his head on the palace walls while shouting: *Varus, give me back my legions!*

In hindsight, it may look obvious that was dangerous to trust a German deserter to lead roman troops in German territory against his own people. The story of this catastrophic defeat serves as an example that every entrepreneur should have in mind: be aware of the conflict of interests when selecting your allies, watching if anyone would win something with your downfall.

Synergies, Possibilities, and Beer.

I hope I made the point about how useful can be to have a local ally and how this benefits your venture. There may be a question still puzzling you, a question that also puzzled me years ago:

What can I, or my business, offer in exchange?

I digress here: Not always you need to offer something in exchange, as the research of Raihani and Bshary - mentioned at the beginning of this chapter - concluded. Still, mutual benefits are a powerful incentive for long-lasting partnerships.

The most attractive of all mutual benefits are synergies. This happens when the combined value or performance of the two companies is greater than the sum of separate individual parts[9].

One example: many tourists we host in Warsaw are also looking for city tours or tailor-made excursions for nearby attractions. By partnering with a city tour operator, we both win. I send my guests to their city tours, while they recommend my hostel for customers inquiring about a room. With reciprocal recommendations, we take out the middleman: internet portals charging up to 15% commission from tour operators and hotels alike.

If more customers and 15% fewer costs are not tempting enough, let's think about the other possibilities, like joint-procurement. If your business and your ally need the same type of supply, why not buy together in a bigger batch, and therefore, with more bargain power?

Example: You need a SEO (*Search Engine Optimization*) specialist for your website. SEO agencies often give good discounts for new clients hiring their services for more than one website. The agency I use has a promotion of *3 websites for the price of 2*. In the same situation, you and your allies can hire an agency together and pay 33% less in total.

Besides all advantages, remember that one great catalyst of coalitions is around for five thousand years, and still works: invite them for a beer.

CHAPTER 5 – DO NOT NEGLECT THE SUPPLY NUMBERS.

Or: Why you should not open another B&B in the Tatra Mountains.

It was a chilly Sunday afternoon. My wife and I met her parents in a café near the main square. While drinking an Irish coffee, her dad asked about how my business was going so far. Later he told me he wanted my opinion - given my experience in the tourism area- about an idea.

He asked what I thought about the plan of acquiring apartments for short-term rental in the region called Podhale, southern Poland, marked by the thrilling Tatra Mountains. To answer this question, I had an internal conflict. This region is our usual choice for winter escapes. We visit there at least one time per year and it has my favorite regional cuisine. For these reasons, my tourist side was very fond of the idea.

However, my entrepreneur side, the side that during years researched the major cities in Poland to decide where to *not* open a business, thought the opposite: another touristic accommodation in the Podhale was a bad idea.

For decades this region attracts tourists, both in the winter holidays - for snow sports and new year parties - and in the summer, for school trips and hikes. Since this is not a new destination, the place has a well-developed hospitality sector.

In summary: the competition the Podhale is **fierce**, and they know what they are doing. Hotels and B&Bs in Zakopane (the winter capital of the region) are operating for generations, and they quickly send inefficient establishments into oblivion. Most of the survivors know very well what they are doing, and they do it properly. It is a hostile terrain for new players, especially inexperienced ones.

My father-in-law thought that another apartment for rent in the mountains was a good idea because the area attracts many tourists. Yes, it draws crowds during winter holidays. However, he forgot that the competition for these tourists is brutal and on a high-level. To start a hospitality venture in Zakopane is equivalent to jump in the cockpit of a Formula 1 to run the *Monaco Grand Prix* with the experience of driving golf carts.

The Siren Song of high-demand & low-barrier markets

Imagine that you live in Amarillo, Texas, and your kids want to open a lemonade stand to make some extra dollars during the summer holidays. Given the hot weather and the number of pedestrians in your street, you tell them this is a great idea: there is a demand for fresh, cold lemonades and they will be the first stand in the neighborhood.

You tell your two children, Joe and Sue, that if they work hard, they may earn money enough to buy a new bicycle!

The children get so excited that you barely need to help

them raise the stand. The first days of operation are booming and they already cover the costs! Even your optimistic perspective of making money enough to buy a bicycle sounds too modest now. But on a Friday afternoon, coming back from work, little Joe runs to you in despair.

Mark, the boy from the house on the other side of the street, also opened a lemonade stand this morning. Your kids had half of their usual customers!

You blame yourself for not seeing the obvious. You blame yourself for giving false hopes to the little ones about a terrific business and new bikes. The hot weather, the pedestrians... how could you not anticipate that the kids' neighbors would soon catch the opportunity to compete with your children?

How could you not see that lemonade stands are a **very-low barrier market?** Just as fishermen seduced by the beautiful siren voice and later sunk by its claws; you, little Joe, and little Sue got seduced by a high-demand market, without perceiving the claws of *low entry barriers.*

The lemonade stand is an example of a *Competitive Shake-out.* George Day, in an article for the Harvard Business Review[10], wrote about it:

High levels of profitability or promises of huge capital gains draw new competitors like magnets. It is axiomatic in economics that every opportunity bears the seed of its own reversal. This is the law of nemesis: Nothing good lasts indefinitely because others will want to share it.

New entrants find little to impede them. When the product or service is easy to imitate, and especially when it uses existing technologies rather than a risky or protected technology, entry barriers are low. [...] Then there is collective surprise when unexpected and unwelcome competitors emerge.

According to the economists Dennis Carlton and Jeffrey Perloff, entry barriers are *anything that prevents an entrepreneur from instantaneously creating a new firm in a market.*

This "anything", this barrier can be:

- High investments required, like in the aerospace industry.
- Intellectual property, as in the pharmaceutical industry.
- Government regulations and concessions, as with port operators.
- Switching barriers, which are the costs that customers need to bear if they want to change providers. This is the case for corporates software like ERPs.
- Zoning laws. When I opened my first hostel, this was a barrier I needed to deal with, since the city zoning laws do not allow hospitality businesses in certain districts.
- Supplier agreements. Exclusivity supplying contracts can complicate for new firms to enter certain markets. That is why; if you want to open a wind turbine manufacturer, you will have a lot of work finding a provider of a mineral called *neodymium*. *Neodymium* providers already have exclusivity contracts to provide the few existing industries.

There are other entry barriers besides those listed above.

The more attractive your market, the more important is to watch out for barriers and do a proper competitive analysis.

To have many customers does not mean much if you have even more competitors.

Before starting your competitive analysis, there are two questions to ask yourself:

1. How to understand my competition and their differentials?
2. How can I match or surpass them while keeping costs controlled?

The answer to the questions above varies from one market to another. In some of them, you will have very specific, easily identifiable competitors. This is the case of the lemonade stand at the beginning of the chapter: the competitor of Joe and Sue was Mark. In other situations, you will have *crossed competition*: companies from other industries disputing with you the same consumer pockets. This happens in the transportation sector, where low-cost airlines compete against bus companies or even against ridesharing phone apps like *BlaBlaCar.*

How to analyze your competition in an unknown land.

There is plenty of material, online and in the printed press, about competitive analysis. Unfortunately, most of it is for entrepreneurs already with business running for years in familiar terrain. If you are reading this book until here, I guess this is not your case. I would bet your project is (or will be) in considerably new surroundings.

Here I will give you a simple but robust 4-step structure to do your competitive analysis while venturing in unfamiliar territory.

1st – Mine the name of every company that will compete with you for customers.

In situations where you are planning business in a new environment, the first step of a competitive analysis is to discover who are your competitors (call me *captain obvious*).

In this first step, it is important to be broad. Select every firm that would pursue the same customers as yours. If you are a brick and mortar business, like a Hotel or a Restaurant, limit the scope by geographic region. If your activity is online, however, geographic variables may not be that important.

Fortunately, in times of big data and the internet, this step got a lot easier. Below I list some tools and techniques helpful to define your competitors:

- Google Maps - After zooming the map to your area, search for companies in your segment, and copy the results to a sheet, to start building your list of competitors.
- Business aggregators – Websites that aggregate and facilitate to find firms in a certain segment. Examples: *Booking.com* for Hotels, *Amazon Local Deals* for retailers, *AgencySpotter* for design and marketing agencies, etc.
- Social Media – In 2019, 91% of the companies in American territory used social media[11]. In other regions, the percentage is smaller but growing. The advantage is that to find your competitors in social network services is easy and intuitive. Just use the *search field*.

- Keywords – Discover competitors by exploring the keywords your customers type in search engines like Google. One little trick is to use the internet navigator in *incognito* mode, type your business segment, and let the browser autocomplete it. For example, when I type *Hostel Warsaw* to discover the competitors of my Hostel, the browser autocomplete tool suggests 3 of my major competitors. I can guess that those three are quite popular among customers using Google, and therefore, important players.

2ˢᵗ – Separate your list by primary, secondary, and tertiary competitors.

After using the tools of the first step, now you have a list of many competitors. The degree that each one of them will dispute customers with you will vary. Therefore, in the second step you separate them into 3 groups:

Primary Competition: Your direct adversaries. They target the same public and have a similar product. In the case of my hostel, they were similar accommodations, with similar customer ratings in the same district and price range, targeting backpackers.

Secondary Competition: They either offer an upgraded/downgraded version of your product or target a different audience. In my case, those were chain hotels (upgraded version of my product) or hostels with considerably lower evaluations than mine (downgraded version).

Tertiary Competition: Here are businesses from different segments than yours, but still could convince potential customers to prefer them instead of your company. Firms selling products vaguely linked by their purpose, like a surfboard and a skateboard competing to be the Christmas gift of Californian teenagers. Identifying these types of competitors is still important.

There is no need to spend much time with tertiary competitors, but by monitoring them, you avoid surprises with unexpected rivalry and discover opportunities for cooperation. Example: RV/Motorhomes rentals are not direct competitors for backpacker hostels. While in sporadic situations, they target the same customers, in others it is possible to cooperate for mutual benefits, like when hostels are a starting point to Motorhome road trips.

3rd – Name tag and SWOT your primary competitors.

One of the biggest mistakes new entrepreneurs do is to stop either at step one or two and think that identifying your competitors is enough. It is not even close to being enough, just like knowing who is the enemy in the battlefield is not enough if you have no idea about the reach of their artillery or the intensity of their air support.

To know who are your primary competitors is an excellent step. But now it is time to understand them. Study them. Know their business almost as good as they know themselves.

One of the greatest tools for this kind of analysis is the *SWOT*. This name of this tool is an acronym where each letter has the following meaning:

- **St**rengths: features giving advantages to your competitor.

- **W**eaknesses: factors that cause disadvantages to your competitor and weaken his market position.
- **O**pportunities: characteristics in the environment or location that your rival can explore.
- **T**hreats: characteristics in the environment that are potential obstacles for your rival.

Just as in the previous steps, the Internet and all information available are helpful here. But if you are opening a business and moving to another country to administrate it, I bet the stakes are high enough to justify *field research*.

When opening my company, I wanted to know deeply about how the major competitors worked. I visited their facilities and made a reservation for my father to sleep in one of them. I read what they offered for customers and observed their physical installations. I was lucky to not be confused with a weird stalker.

One very important point to understand the strengths and weaknesses of your opponents is to read what the customers write about them. For hostels, for example, portals like TripAdvisor or Google Hotels have hundreds of customer opinions available. I tabulated them to understand in which points my competitors over-performed (their strengths) and where they underperformed (their weaknesses). In a broad definition, the strengths of my rivals are threats to my business, while their weaknesses uncover opportunities for my company.

Overall, I consider reading customer reviews of your primary adversaries one of the easiest, cheapest, and most efficient ways to discover untapped opportunities.

Here is the SWOT analysis that I made from one of my competitors (I substituted the actual name for a fictitious one):

PatchHoliday Hostel

Strengths: Prime location; good reviews in internet portals; trendy bar driving guests and creating additional revenue streams; large size, allowing economies of scale, and possibility to accommodate large groups.

Weaknesses: High fixed costs (expensive building rent); young and volatile team, resulting in a constant need for recruitment and training.

Opportunities: Possibility of establishing an in-house tour desk to generate additional revenue, possible acquisition of neighboring smaller hostels for economy of scale.

Threats: The owner of the building may opt to not extend the rental agreement, therefore displacing the business to a less favorable location. The attractiveness of the region can attract chain hostels, with lower costs and enormous marketing power.

Just for curiosity, two of the threats I identified proved to be true. In 2019, the owner of the building where *PatchHoliday* operated decided to not extend the rental agreement. Simultaneously, the region witnessed the arrival of a big German hospitality chain, with a Hostel two times larger than any competitor.

4th – *Do a comprehensive pricing scrutiny of your primary competitors*

In 2018, I approached another business to inquire about a

potential acquisition. He had a budget hotel, and I noticed he was running at a very low occupation.

Knowing that if I questioned him about his lower occupation, he would turn defensive and maybe create some excuse, I decided to inquire about his pricing: how much he charged for a night in a double room. The price he told me was almost 30% higher than the market average. No wonder his hotel was empty. When I asked why such a high price, he answered: *This is what I think it is fair for the quality of our services.*

Here is one painful truth:

Your opinion of what is a *fair price* is irrelevant.

This is especially true if you are an entrepreneur in a new environment, since your idea of *fairness* can detach from reality.

Who will decide if your price is fair or not are your customers. They will do it after comparing you with the competition. Therefore, anticipate it and do a pricing comparison yourself, during the competitive analysis.

For pricing research, spreadsheets are your best friends.

Resist the impulse of *only taking a peek* at your primary competitors' prices. In the unlikely scenario where everyone in your market sells only one product with one price, maybe you will not need a spreadsheet. But if assortment and prices vary, registering the changes helps to compare *apples with apples* and identify pricing trends.

Since your primary competitors have a product and target similar to you, to monitor their prices is essential to define your own pricing strategies. This is not advice to just follow the competition, but to avoid prices that scary your customers. If you are an entrepreneur in a new region, if the prices are all equal customers will favor the businesses they already know.

Sometimes, business owners discover that their prices were unrealistic and, to be competitive, they would need to decrease prices to an unprofitable level. If this is your case (I hope not), the solutions are to look for cost-reductions or features that make your product more attractive, justifying a higher price.

Trend identification: the additional benefit of pricing scrutiny.

When I was planning my first business, I spent 12 months registering the prices of my primary competitors. Every Friday I examined their prices and recorded them in a spreadsheet. The entire process took around 30 minutes, weekly. After one year, I had near two thousand price points and a complete outlook of the pricing trends. I knew the prices peak in July and sharply decreased from November to February. Thanks to this knowledge, I postponed the business opening to the first semester, as to avoid the worst time of the year.

The most obvious way to know your competition

I left this at the end of the chapter because it is useful only if your business is open and running. After we get used to online market research, burying our heads in Excel sheets, often we forget a source literally in our front door: our customers.

Arthur Weiss, managing director of the UK-Based

consultancy *Aware*, said in an interview for the portal Inc.com[12]:

Speaking to customers is one of the best (and cheapest) ways of gathering actual information on competitors. Whenever you win a new customer, find out who they used before, and why they switched to you (i.e. The reason for their dissatisfaction with the previous supplier). Do the same when you lose a customer - identify what they preferred about your competitor. If you gather enough of these stories, you'll get a clear idea on what competitors offer that customers view as preferable. You can then adjust your own offering to beat that of the competitor.

Asking your customers about your competition likely will make a positive impression on them – it shows you care about their preferences – and also will allow discovering a type of competitor difficult to detect: the failed ones. *Why* you should care about the failures is a discussion for the next chapter. For now, I leave you with a summary of the steps for making proper competitive research to your enterprise:

Summary:

1st – Mine the name of every company that will compete with you for customers.

2st – Separate your list by primary, secondary, and tertiary competitors.

3rd – Name tag and SWOT your primary competitors.

4th – Do a comprehensive pricing scrutiny of the competition.

CHAPTER 6 – AVOID PATHS LEADING TO BUSINESS DESTRUCTION.

Via Negativa and the Pseudo-Areopagite

Dionysius was a neo-platonic theologian from the VI century. He synthesized the concept of *Via Negativa* (Latin term meaning *Path of Negation*).

According to this idea, if we admit the existence of a supreme being above the reason of all humans, it is impossible for anyone to define him. Definitions are, after all, imposing limits to the existence. Since we cannot tell what God *is* because it is out of our capacity, the only possibility to describe this Supreme Being is to say what *he is not*.

While Dionysius was the first to describe the notion of *Via Negativa*, the Old Testament and ancient thinkers like Saint Augustine of Hippo used the core notion[13]. Brilliance aside, Dionysius was not very original, since his name (*The Aeropagite*) is actually a pseudonym taken from a man from centuries before. That is why he is frequently called *Dionysius the Pseudo-Areopagite*. Not a flattering way to refer to the man who summarized a concept used not only in theology but in heuristic.

The Survivorship Bias

During university, I worked part time at an investment brokerage firm. An efficient tool to sell quotas of riskier funds were a dozen slides with time spams ranging from ten to twenty years.

Virtually every share or hedge fund in this time span had positive (and above inflation) returns. This sequence of slides was enough to convince potential customers that in the "long-term", risky investments pay off.

It was flawed reasoning. Almost deceitful, to be honest, even though I do not plead guilty, but just ignorant – I had little knowledge of selection biases.

In a market where either you have positive returns or your investors will withdraw and liquidate your fund, it is clear how misleading were those slides. By choosing a 10-year period, with only the current investment options, they filtered out bankrupt funds, and the investors had no idea about the possible failures they could face.

This is what we call *survivorship bias*. Every time you see *solid* investments with positive returns over decades, you are biasing observation by accidentally filtering out failures.

This treacherous bias turns you into a fool, making poor decisions in financial, personal, and business dimensions.

To discover the good path, first eliminate the paths leading to failure.

I first illustrated the concepts of *Via Negativa* and the *Survivorship Bias* because together they are the foundation for the argument I will show in the next pages.

In the previous chapter, you learned that a comprehensive competitive analysis is an important step to build a business. To do this analysis, the SWOT (*Strengths, Weaknesses, Opportunities, and Threats*) matrix is an incredible tool. However, when you analyze your existing competitors, the observed *weaknesses* and *threats* often are far from the worst scenarios. Otherwise, those competitors would already be out of the market.

A similar bias happened during World War II, when American military specialists thought they should reinforce planes in the wings and tails because that is where fighters had bullet holes - while engines of returning planes were mostly intact-, not realizing that the aircrafts shot in the engine never came back[14]. When you analyze the *weaknesses* of your current competitors, you are just observing bullet holes in the wings.

In his book *Antifragile*, Taleb points out that the best way for a person or company to not only survive but prosper in a crisis is to first decrease his disadvantages. A disadvantage (we can also call them *fragilities*) comprises everything increasing your vulnerability to risk and volatility.

Know the shortcomings of failed businesses, so the past does not repeat itself.

The reason which I started this chapter introducing a heuristic concept (*Via Negativa*), and a logical bias (*Survivorship Bias*) is because **knowing what kills a business is equally (or even more) important than understanding what makes it succeed**.

The first step to success is to survive. Had I never learned about the weaknesses of similar companies to mine, I would not be writing those pages about entrepreneurship abroad, because my own business would be dead.

I understand that researching bankrupt businesses and their *Causa Mortis* is not a motivating task. Every entrepreneur wants to keep a fair dose of optimism to keep going forward. But do not let optimism plays against you. To discover the route for triumph, the first step is to eliminate the paths leading to failure. Work with multiple scenarios and seek to get rid of your weaknesses in each of them. By eliminating the detrimental routes, your chances of choosing the correct door are much higher.

CHAPTER 7 – UNCONTROLLED CHANGES WILL ALWAYS EXIST. SEEK TO THRIVE WITH THEM.

How Nassim Nicholas Taleb Saved My Business

It is not an overstatement to say that I could go bankrupt — like many of my competitors — during the 2020 Covid19 crisis.

One year before the pandemic starts, I decided to expand my hostel in Warsaw, and I needed additional resources.

Loans are relatively cheap in Poland. Even young and high-risk companies like mine can find rates around 7% per year. For some time, I considered taking a loan to finance our expansion. However, after a re-evaluation, instead of taking bank money, I preferred to bring new partners. They would own a good portion of the business, although I would still be the main shareholder.

Colleagues and family asked me if instead of bringing in new shareholders, would not be better simply to take a loan, since the rates were attractive. They even listed the benefits of taking credit instead of new partners:

- The peace of mind of not risking other people's money.
- No need to explain to anyone about my decisions, or company results.
- Reduced legal expenses.

Despite these advantages, I took another way because of two concepts from Nassim Taleb: *Antifragility*, that I will use in this chapter, and *Skin in the Game*, which will come in a later section.

To introduce the first concept, Taleb wrote:

Some things benefit from shocks; they thrive and grow when exposed to volatility, randomness, disorder, and stressors and love adventure, risk, and uncertainty. Yet, despite the ubiquity of the phenomenon, there is no word for the exact opposite of fragile. Let us call it antifragile. Antifragility is beyond resilience or robustness. The resilient resists shocks and stays the same; the antifragile gets better. This property is behind everything that has changed with time: evolution, culture, ideas, revolutions, political systems, technological innovation, cultural and economic success, corporate survival, good recipes (say, chicken soup or steak tartare with a drop of cognac), the rise of cities, cultures, legal systems, equatorial forests, bacterial resistance ... even our own existence as a species on this planet.

Bringing in new partners made my business more *antifragile* than taking money from banks for 2 reasons:

1 — In a serious crisis (like the COVID-19 pandemic) that

devastates tourism, I do not need to pay dividends if I have no profits. On the other side, if I take a bank loan, I need to pay the installments or they execute the company.

2 — The non-obligation of shareholder payments preserves the company cash flow during a crisis. Therefore, it helps it to survive and gives time to adapt to the new market conditions. This adaptation takes the form of new technologies and processes, increasing efficiency, and cutting costs. One example is the deal we broke recently with a ride-sharing company, reducing the costs of guest transfers by more than 40%.

We not only survived the crisis – what is already something, since local touristic businesses tend to be fragile – but we are leaving it stronger than before.

The dangers of technological, economic, and environmental changes

Journalists and economists called the 2020 economical troubles a *once-in-a-lifetime* crisis. Journalists and economists also called the 2008 market-crash a *once-in-a-lifetime* crisis.

I cannot be anything except puzzled by the fact that a 35-year old like me already witnessed two *once-in-a-lifetime* crisis. Some people from my generation think we are unlucky. However, our parents witnessed the cold war and the oil crisis; our grandparents' two world wars; and our great-grandparents, the Spanish flu, and the 1929 economic collapse.

My generation is not unlucky. The truth is that journalists use the term *once-in-a-lifetime crisis* for crisis happening more than once in a lifetime. Or maybe they are referring to the life span of cats.

With the understatement of how frequent crisis are, entrepreneurs think that is worthless to prepare for a collapse that may not come. This is a mistake.

A mistake that creates an advantage for outsiders like us. You can use your previous experience to add layers to the risk assessment. One example: I am very used to the risk represented by currency changes, since Brazil changed it 5 times in the last four decades. In Poland, frequently arises the subject of changing the national currency (*Zloty*) for the Euro. Very few people understand the risks associated with such change.

A foreigner entrepreneur should use to his advantage the knowledge of an outer environment and create a competitive advantage by being ready for a risk that his competitors are not even aware it exists.

You cannot predict the next crisis, but you can rehearse for it.

A simple but efficient way to assess the risks for your business is the *Impact vs Likehood matrix.* Remember that here we are discussing uncontrollable risks, so while you cannot suppress a crisis, you can prepare your business to survive (and thrive) on it.

The first step to use this matrix is to draw a chart where the X-Axis measures impact – be it profit margin at risk or any other suitable measure, and the Y-Axis is measuring *likelihood*. Attribute the *likelihood* of catastrophic events with extra care, since humans underestimate the chances of calamity (unless they just went through one). One common way to attribute likelihood is to observe how frequently the event happens. However this may lead to non-detection of rare-but-not-impossible situations – Black Swans, as Nassim Taleb calls them.

To detect Black Swans, the best way is to brainstorm every conceivable and possible adversity, accident, or disaster. Since you are an entrepreneur far away, bring the knowledge baggage from your land and sum the known, old risks to the ones of the new place. Brainstorm together with other entrepreneurs or neighboring residents, if possible.

Once you have a relevant poll of unpleasant situations, divide them in the matrix below, according to both their likelihood and impact.

Likelihood	High	Casual accidents. Opportunities for improvement.	Disasters. Build protective measures against them.
	Low	Fly in the soup.	Rare catastrophes. Insure and mitigate their impacts.
		Low	High
		Impact	

Fly in the soup: The name of the quadrant with low probability and low impact is self-explanatory. When you have a fly in your soup, you just take another bowl. You do not install expensive security systems or create detailed mitigation protocols for the problems of this quadrant because the investment would far exceed the avoided losses. But be sure that what you place in the *fly in the soup quadrant* are truly low-probability events, because even though their impact is low, if it happens frequently, it will pile up and turn into a money and time-consuming issue.

Casual accidents: The frequent bumps in your entrepreneurial road have their place in the high-likelihood, low-impact quadrant. Example? When I started my business in Poland, it was difficult to hire. A near-zero unemployment rate can be a risk for employers, even though I personally prefer that instead of high unemployment. Each expense from the recruiting effort was not significant when isolated, but summed all the costs of training, job ads, understaffing and uncertainty, it became considerable. Therefore, it was a management challenge, and a chance for improvement, something valid for most problems written in the *Casual accidents* quadrant.

Disasters: The high-impact, high-probability risks are the ones we actively avoid. Just after university, I moved to Santiago, the Chilean capital. The region is one of the most earthquake-prone in the world, registering a third of all tremors above 8.5 of magnitude. Earthquakes have a high-likelihood in Chile, and their impact can be calamitous. Consequently, Chile is one of the leading countries in anti-seismic technology. When we talk about uncontrollable but frequent disasters, the effort is to mitigate their effects when they happen, because sooner than later they will.

Rare catastrophes:

In this quadrant are situations like global market crashes,

LEVI BORBA

pandemics, or Vulcan eruptions causing an airspace lockdown in half-continent (the Eyjafjallajökull did this in 2010).

I left the *rare catastrophes* quadrant at last because people often neglect it. While *flies in the soup* do not have the impact necessary to demand attention, and both *casual accidents* and likely *disasters* are easily identifiable because of their frequency, we, humans, struggle to understand the likelihood of *rare catastrophes.*

There is even a name for this cognitive brain flaw: *normalcy bias.* According to the research from Esther Inglis-Arkell, near 70% of people display such bias[15].

At the risk of sounding repetitive, I will tell you again: To thrive, first a business must survive. Online commerce behemoths like eBay or Amazon are companies that survived the 2000 e-commerce bubble burst.

Black swans like enormous Vulcan eruptions or virus mutations are impossible to predict. Therefore, the best countermeasure is to get rid of the fragilities and catalysts of negative impact. Build diversified income streams, create redundancies, and avoid risks that can wipe out your company. These are some ways to build an antifragile enterprise.

If you want your business to survive one hundred years, events that happen once in a century should alarm you.

How to be prepared: Innovation-Readiness

The top quadrants of the *likelihood vs impact* matrix are easy to identify. We know when *casual accidents* and *likely disasters* occur because they happen frequently, just like earthquakes in Chile.

How should a business respond to them? Here I would like to suggest two ways, both intimately related: Spearhead Innovation and Combat Readiness.

Spearhead Innovation

Spearhead innovation, also called cutting-edge or vanguard innovation, are the methods and technologies at the knowledge frontier of your industry.

You should pay attention to whatever is at the boundary of your industry, although not everything there is useful. In fact, a lot of the *vanguard* innovation will fall into oblivion because they do not add value enough to compensate for the investment. However, what is not worthy today can be a lifesaver (or business-saver) in case of drastic environmental changes or likely disasters.

In my area, hospitality, one example is the high-tech automation intended to reduce the payroll of budget hotels. With those technologies, it would be perfectly possible to run an entire hotel with near no one at the front desk. In Poland, where employment costs are not high, and customers enjoy the help of a receptionist, this would not be profitable. At least not in normal conditions.

Then came 2020, together with the Pandemic and the need for social distancing.

Fortunately, I have the costume of reserve between 1 to 2 hours per week to read about the vanguard practices and cutting-edge technologies in my field. When the pandemic forced us to implement social distancing measures, we immediately substituted the airport transfer service to vouchers, which they could use to do their transfers in cars adapted to the new sanitary regulations.

Mark Achler, an adjunct lecturer of innovation and entrepreneurship at Kellogg, once told[16]:

Most companies spend decades building up a core business and the bureaucracy to support that core business. [This is, after all, the proven strategy that got the organization where it is today]. "But it also means that everybody's time and attention is focused on that core business. So if you don't create urgency around innovation, then it's really easy to put it off, [...]. Innovation's not one- or two-year chunks, you've got to have a three- to five-year time horizon, because it takes time to source and vet ideas.

Mark Achler has a point. It takes time to source and understand the leading innovations useful to your business. Do not wait until it forces you to innovate, because it may be too late. But also do not revolutionize for the sake of it. Instead, the approach I support is to discover regularly what is the innovation spearhead, cutting-edge knowledge of your industry.

Combat Readiness

The Spokane Trophy is an award given every year to the ship of the United States Pacific Fleet with the best overall level of combat readiness. Time is critical during military actions. That is why the period needed to be ready for combat decreased from months during medieval times to minutes nowadays.

Maybe you ask why the previous paragraph is in a book about entrepreneurship.

An excellent business book I read is from an author called Michael Abrashoff[17], from where I took this important lesson: *Constantly plan for "What if" situations. Be battle-ready and handled by the most highly prepared, motivated and respected staff.*

Remember the Spokane trophy I mentioned above? Michael Abrashoff, before becoming a business author, was a navy captain, and he turned one of the worst-performing ships in the navy into a winner of this trophy, and one of the most combat-ready destroyers of the US Navy.

For navy ships, a torpedo coming in their direction is a *likely disaster*. To face a hostile fleet in suspicious distances is a *casual accident*. A ship captain must be ready to face the top row of the *likelihood vs impact* matrix. Just like an entrepreneur can face market changes or economic crisis. If a battle is likely to happen, prepare your business, train your staff to act, protect your financial resources and build the operational capabilities to launch protective counter-measures. By acting in this sequence, you will better conduct your business – or your ship – through combat.

In other words: Do not spend your time wishing for uncontrollable turmoils to never occur. Aim to be ready for them, just like if they were going to happen in the next day, or the coming hours.

Cash flow protection: Working capital is for business what water is for an aquarium.

Imagine that your business is a running-water aquarium, with a constant inflow of water from a tap, and outflow through holes in the lower side. Your expenditures is the water flowing out and your revenue is the inflow from the tap. In normal times, the inflow should be equal or bigger than the outflow, so you can take the excess water and use in other aquariums. This water surplus is your profit.

If your tap stops flowing, either you close the holes quick enough to avoid the aquarium to dry, or have a water reserve.

Coming back to business, the expenditure holes are rents, bills, salaries, debts, etc.

Avoiding unnecessary debt and adopting flexible contracts (beneficial to your business during a crisis) are two of the most efficient ways to turn your business *antifragile*.

If you have flexible contracts, you can close them quickly enough. When the 2020 pandemic crisis started, one of the first actions surviving entrepreneurs took across the world (including me) was to renegotiate agreements, intending to close the bleeding holes.

Not always you can seal the holes fast enough to not let your aquarium go dry. This is when you need to have a water reserve. In business, we call this a *working capital reserve*. This reserve will guarantee your survival during the months of no revenue inflow. In April, during the apex of the 2020 crisis in Poland, I saw an incredible amount of businesses go bankrupt just because they could not survive a single month without revenue.

Have a *working capital* reserve. This can be the difference between a surviving enterprise and one going belly up.

CHAPTER 8 – WHEN IT IS TIME TO REINVENT YOUR BUSINESS?

Why the world's greatest investor changed his own doctrine

During college, I worked in a local brokerage firm. The investment advisors there admired some financial market names in the same way little-league basketball players idolize Michael Jordan. As I remember, Warren Buffett frequently topped the rankings of the most commented *big-shot* investors.

His clear money doctrine and consistency across decades made specialists turn his name into a common defense of *buy and hold*[18] strategies. From his investment philosophy, one axiom was singular, because it pointed out where Buffett does *not* invest: Tech companies.

In a letter from 1986[19] addressed to the shareholders of his conglomerate, the mega-investor stated he would not invest in technology and instead favor *simple businesses*. In the same letter, he explained that *simple* means *easy to understand*. In other words, traditional, century-long industries.

Warren Buffett kept the promise of his letter for decades, preferring traditional and *simple* sectors like food & beverages

(*Coca-Cola* and *Dairy Queen* are in his portfolio), railways, and mining.

Until 2016.

Thirty years after the letter denying investment in tech companies, Buffet acquired massive *Apple Inc.* shares. In a short period, he became the second-biggest shareholder of the company founded by Steve Jobs, with near 20 billion dollars invested.

What made Warren Buffett adjust his mind?

Apple changed with the years and turned into a company better known for its customer loyalty and premium brand than technological complexities. It became simpler, more similar to a consumer-product corporation than a volatile and complicated tech business.

The changes Apple went through to turn into the current success resulted in Warren Buffett changing his paradigm and finding a great investment opportunity. Significant enough to guarantee the American investor over 40 billion dollars in profit.

Prisoner of its past success

In 2009, Nokia was the 5th most valuable brand in the world. Their phones were an object of desire everywhere. One year before I bought a used N80, and even with few scratches, it looked so much better than the competing phones.

Fast-forward to 2014 and Nokia dropped to 98th place in the ranking[20]. Two other phone makers dominated the market: Apple and Samsung, respectively, the first and seventh-most valuable brands of the planet.

More than half of all profits from the mobile-phone industry went to Nokia in 2007. In 2013, they were in such a critical situation that Microsoft came to the rescue.

Nokia had a hardware-centered business model and underestimated the software revolution caused by the birth of smartphones. Apple came with the iPhone in 2007, to which Samsung quickly responded with their Galaxy series powered by the open-source *Android*. Meanwhile, Nokia rowed against the tide, betting on the superiority of its hardware to compensate for software deficiencies.

Nokia was a prisoner of its past success, and with the dawn of a new era, they hesitated too long to adapt.

The myth of Innovation and Adaptation as mutually exclusive

In previous chapters, you read about entrepreneurs seeking the cutting-edge knowledge of their fields. By being aware of the industry vanguard innovations, it is possible to resort to them if needed.

While ***innovation*** awareness is desirable, it should not exclude the prospect for ***adaptation***. Business graduates may think that the two terms are mutually exclusive. Others, on the opposite side, might think they mean the same thing. Both are wrong, because while they are different, both can be part of the ethos of the same enterprise.

Innovation is often disruptive, sparked by creativity, and validated by frequent testing with a high failure rate. Adaptation, on the other side, is evidence-based, sparked by experience and knowledge of different scenarios and has a lower failure rate.

With those two definitions in mind, it is easier for an entrepreneur far from home to be innovative instead of adaptive. When I moved to Poland to open my business, I had plenty of ideas that I wanted to test, but very limited knowledge of the terrain to design different scenarios. There is a way to overturn this disadvantage.

Commit not with an idea only, but with a profitable business that pays for itself.

Especially in the technology world, the widespread promotion of innovation shadows adaptation. Often the success of adaptation from previous business models is wrongly attributed to pure innovation. Few examples:

- Before becoming a leader in internet streaming, Netflix was a DVD-by-mail rental company. Their idea of delivering entertainment with convenience was always the same, but adapted to the progress of internet bandwidth.
- With the demise of analogic photography, Kodad nearly disappeared after more than a century of activity. It re-emerged later serving her core customers (photographers and film-makers) differently: with hardware and digital tools for image licensing.
- During a half-century, UK residents used the *Yellow Pages* publications to consult local phones and addresses. With the Internet, the publishers went online and turned into *Yell.com*, the UK's leading online business directory.

- On its way to global expansion, Starbucks did not bet always in the same successful formula used in the USA. They developed taste profile analyses to adapt their products to each region, to the point that in China they adopted ancient tea house practices intrinsic to the local culture[21].

Reading the above examples, you may think it is all about *innovation* instead of *adaptation*. But see how none of the companies mentioned changed their target customers, or how their products are still related. It is not a case of completely changing their business, but adapting to new environments (like Starbucks in China) or technological changes (like Netflix, Yellow Pages, and Kodak).

The same kind of adaptation that brought prosperity for the above examples (and to Samsung), lacked at Nokia. The Finnish company insisted that design and hardware superiority – with all the heavy investments to acquire it - could protect them against the mobile app revolution.

The idea of "we invested too much to change our ways now" translates into one of the most dangerous business traps: *the sunk cost fallacy.*

Forget Sunk Costs. Be Like Water.

Imagine you moved to a new state, on the other side of the country. You just took a loan to refurbish an old building, turning it into state-of-the-art rental apartments to host MBA students from the nearby university. It is a campus city, and you are the only prime-accommodation supplier, so profits are near guaranteed.

One day, you receive the news that the state university will move all the executive programs to the capital, leaving only undergraduate courses in your city. Undergrads have less money, so either you lower your rental prices for unprofitable levels, or give back the building and close your rental venture.

While the second decision may sound the most logical, a fair share of the entrepreneurs would still take the first, using two justifications:

1. It might happen that after some time, the university decision is reversed and the MBA courses return, together with the customers.
2. The money and time invested are too high to just give up.

While the first justification, if based on factual evidence, is acceptable, the second is not logic. It means to keep losing every month just to not "lose" the initial amount invested. Even this phrase that I just wrote makes little sense, because this thought – called *the sunk cost fallacy* – does not make sense either.

Still, executives and even governments take decisions based on this fallacy, which we also name it *The Concorde Fallacy.* The name originates in the insistence of the British and French governments to fund the unprofitable operations of the supersonic airplane for years, just because it was expensive to develop it.

Nokia, the Concorde or our fictitious rental-apartment business are examples of fallacies and biases blocking the adaptation to new environmental, economic, and technological realities.

There is a quote useful (and thought-provoking) for entrepreneurs facing changes and seeking adaptation.

Be like water making its way through cracks. [...] If you put water into a cup, it becomes the cup. You put water into a bottle and it becomes the bottle. You put it in a teapot; it becomes the teapot.

This quote could be from Warren Buffett when he changed his 3-decade long rule and invested in Apple Inc. It could be from Apple themselves when the company explored the still uncertain mobile-software business. Or even from Starbucks, when they invested in tea shops to expand to China.

The author, though, was the martial artist Bruce Lee.[22]

CHAPTER 9 – UNDERSTAND THE LOCALS UNTIL ALMOST BECOME ONE OF THEM. BUT KEEP YOUR BAGGAGE.

The Lebanese Secret

Brazil hosts one of the largest Lebanese diasporas in the world. This should not come as a surprise, since Brazil – a country made by immigrants - also hosts some of the biggest communities of Syrian, Japanese, Pole and Italian descendants. But there is one factor that differs the Brazilian-Lebanese community from all the other diasporas in the region.

They are much more successful than the rest. Despite being only 4% of the total population, they are tremendously overrepresented in the political and business sphere. Example? Between 1982 and 2017, of the 11 mayors of São Paulo, 4 had Lebanese origins.

The achievements of the Levantine[23] diaspora in South-America are similar to what we see in other parts of the world. Nonetheless, Brazilian-Lebanese's make a curious case because they outperform various immigrant groups that arrived at the same time and with similar conditions. What made them so successful?

Nassim Taleb (also a Lebanese) provides an interesting answer:

The idea is that in a natural setting, anything natural, anything organic, anything biological, up to a point, reacts a lot better to stressors than without... a little bit of adversity results in a little bit more performance in anything.

Adversities are natural in the Levant. Coming from a region threatened by invasions, natural catastrophes, and economical collapses, they developed the tools to thrive under tension. Moving to Brazil in a time of regime changes, economic turmoil and even a civil war[24], they faced similar instabilities, scary things for most people, but just a normal day for the Lebanese, which prospered in the chaos.

A Toltec in Vietnam

Curious about Lebanese success and relation with their experience back home, I asked other foreigners how their homeland skills helped them to succeed far away.

The investment consultant/ Gilbert Dominguez is an unusual example. He is a member of the Indigenous people from Central America, in the region once inhabited by the Toltecs. He moved to Vietnam, and while the two cultures are distinct, with virtually no historical contact, some of its traces helped him in his new place.

The Vietnamese culture shares many of my same values. They are all for individual expression, perhaps even individual achievement, but not for individual interest over the interest of the whole.

Vietnam is a collectivist culture, just as pre-Colombian civilizations like the Toltecs. As a result of this similarity, the *Hofstede* ranking of *Individualism vs Collectivism* places Vietnam and Mexico with similarly low scores (20 and 30 respectively) in a ranking where the higher means more individualistic. Curiously, Mexico shares a border with one of the most individualistic countries in the World, the United States, which scores a whopping 91. In this aspect, Mexico is more similar to the Asian nation than to his northern neighbor.

Western thinking? Won't work here.

In the previous example, likely Gilbert Dominguez never raised major objections from the Vietnamese by behaving in his natural way. This is because while distant, the Central-American indigenous culture had characteristics close to the Vietnamese attitude.

It is not always like that. Sometimes, even though your childhood nurtures useful skills and abilities, it also brings what I call *inertial antagonism.*

The inertial antagonism is the reaction people (sometimes, entire communities) have when they conform to a long-standing problem and do not know how to overcome it. Even though people know that there is a problem, they just prefer to keep the status quo instead of trying another way to solve it.

The major root of inertial antagonism are preconceptions that people have against foreign methods. Sometimes preconceptions have factual basis and avoid disasters. A famous case was of the Brazilian coach Vanderlei Luxemburgo. One of the two most victorious coaches in Brazilian football, he accepted to train Real Madrid in 2004. It was a squad filled with some of the most successful players of the time, nicknamed *Galacticos*. Luxemburgo adopted techniques like the *quadrado mágico (magical square)*, a very offensive, Brazilian-minted formation. Native specialists warned that such an offensive style could not fit European fields. One year later, Real Madrid fired him.

When locals tell you that *the techniques from your land will not work here*, listen to them and analyze their objections carefully. If there are shreds of evidence that your once successful methods will not work, rethink your ways. But if there is no evidence of failure besides the typical inertial antagonism, then go forward. Just like Ward Chartier.

Mr. Chartier is a seasoned expatriate. For 14 years, he lived in five different countries, including the Far East. When I asked about the conflicts created by bringing foreign methods and cultural characteristics, he answered me:

We, Americans, have the unfortunate reputation of being arrogant and loud. My personality is neither, but I still remained aware of the general perception and acted to avoid it. In addition, I avoided slang, spoke slower than my usual moderate pace of speech, and enunciated clearly.

A few people derided my methods and management tools as "Western thinking. Won't work here." My methods and tools were actually a hybrid of East and West, which I explained, but some remained intransigent. Let them think what they wish. My results were financially and operationally successful for the benefit of my customers and employers.

There are two points in the answer of Mr. Chartier that I would like to highlight:

1.   When confronted with a negative preconception from the locals – the idea that Americans are arrogant and loud – he avoided giving any sign of these undesired characteristics.

2.   When people doubted his battle-tested techniques, he did not see further evidence that they would not work there. His colleagues just had inertial antagonism. So he applied his methods and proved by the result that they work.

Point 2 is a fruitful approach to deal with reactions like *"the techniques from your land will not work here"*.

Regarding point 1, avoiding to give ground to some preconceptions is prudent, but only if they are *negative*. If they are *positive* presumptions, be aware that you have a good reputation to justify. One example is the natural expectation that British and Swiss citizens will be punctual.

Even if it is just a stereotype, it is positive, so worth keeping it, right?

Assimilate, but keep your tools sharp

I started this chapter with the story behind the Lebanese success in Brazil. Used to political and economic storms, they prospered in a volatile place on the other side of the globe thanks to inherited skills.

Skills are often like muscles: after stressing your skills, you have an overcompensation (or myelination) and become sharper on them. On the other side, if you do not use a certain muscle, it atrophies and loses tonus. Just like your abilities. Failing to recall languages we studied during school and never used later serves as proof.

Just like the Lebanese, Brazilians became used to chaos. My generation was born during a decade-long economic pandemonium when the country reached 80% of inflation. Not per decade, not by year or semester, but per month. This developed a unique characteristic of Brazilians that in Portuguese we call *Jeitinho*. It is the ability to bootstrap ways to run a project while dribbling problems, like Ronaldinho escaping from defenders.

On some occasions, the *jeitinho* is used to create scams. In others, however, it creates billionaire - and legal- startups. I am sure you heard about one called Instagram.

Often I saw Brazilians losing this skill when they moved to developed countries. That's why, even living in a stable country, I enjoy discussing business and helping colleagues in Brazil with their problems. Problems that I do not witness in Europe. This is a way to keep sharp my native skill to survive in volatility while living in a non-volatile economy.

If tomorrow Poland has problems similar to what I saw in Brazil (hopefully not), the understanding of survival in instability will be helpful.

Adapt to the culture of your host, but do not let its comforts make you too soft. Do not take *what is better* for granted. The tools you gained during your previous experiences? Keep them sharp.

CHAPTER 10 - HOW TO NOT WASTE MONEY IN YOUR BUSINESS ABROAD

If you spend holidays abroad occasionally, at least once you wasted money on something, and later realized how easy was to avoid the mistake. Maybe you ate the courtesy bread-basket in a Portuguese restaurant, without knowing it was not for free. Maybe during your last ski trip, you took a taxi to the slopes, just to discover later that there was a free shuttle for anyone with a ski pass. Tourists have a fair share of *oh, why I did not see this before!*, followed by the regret of losing a few bucks.

The same happens with a surprising frequency to entrepreneurs abroad. This leakage of small sums, drops of money wasted that at the end of the year could fill a bucket, is the difference between a profit and loss.

It gets worse when a project has deep pocketed investors, as more and more startups are in this age of venture capital. If scarcity is a catalyst to optimize investments, abundance can make it dumber. It is not rare to see tech companies with barely a place in the market and not making any profit, throwing lavish celebrations because of some vanity metric (like page views or clicks).

The best way to avoid the *tourist mentality* and not waste money on trip mistakes is to **not** withdrawal your maximum holiday budget[25]. In the same way, when starting a business, do not look at all your raised capital as *disposable capital*. Countless companies could avoid debacle if only they reserved a part of their initial money for disasters. To have this financial backup for emergencies is the first step, so once you made it, the next stage is to tap the leaks where the money drops out.

How to avoid leaks when you are investing abroad?

Understand what is expensive and assimilate the costs

In my first book - *Moving Out, Working Abroad and Keeping Your Sanity* – I wrote about how specific advice for living abroad is tricky since countries are full of particularities.

So when I tell you to understand what is expensive in your new location, it means *to do relative cost research*. Visit tools like Numbeo or Expatistan[26] and check how prices differentiate between your new and old markets.

This is not time wasted, but invested. The money you will save will compensate each second.

Does your new country have expensive square meters, making the office space maintenance costly? Invest in remote work. Since the 2020 pandemic, technological tools to facilitate home office have unlocked this option to several new areas.

Is it difficult - or expensive - to hire people for support functions? Outsource it. Websites like Upwork, Fiverr, and Freelancer make it easy to find specialists for almost anything possible to do remotely. But be careful to not outsource your core activities – later I will write more on this.

Are the paperwork costs too high? Are you wasting too much time signing and sending forms? Use an electronic signature and avoid lines in the post-office and public offices.

Are you spending afternoons trying to understand new regulations in your sector? Look for someone that already deals with them and ask for an ad hoc consultation. LinkedIn is a good place to find specialists.

This last instruction goes in line with a thing I learned in a hard way:

Do not let the lack of knowledge destroy your leverages.

Or:

Do not be fooled.

Dishonest taxi drivers cheat tourists by doing longer paths because the victim lacks familiarity to realize all the unnecessary turns. Deceitful mechanics will test the client's understanding to see how far they can invent problems and rip off. In these and many other situations, your lack of knowledge destroys your customer leverages and creates the money leaks mentioned at the beginning of this chapter.

If you are opening a business, potential providers will assume that you have money to invest, plus the need to purchase services and materials. While I believe most people have good intentions, a capitalized entrepreneur is attractive for predators disguised as partners. When starting my business, I fell prey to a SEO (*Search Engine Optimization*) agency that charged me an absurd amount for very subpar service.

Realizing how money leaked out to SEO agencies, I learned the subject and discovered better alternatives. Digression: In fact, I found SEO so interesting that I created a new website just to test the things I was learning. Cool stuff, besides saving some money by assimilating this cost, I discovered a new hobby and gained an extra skill.

Be humble. Before spending hours planning targets, invest time in chats with more experienced (in your market and location) entrepreneurs. Besides discovering details like the best suppliers, you will also see how the successful ones in your field are: what are their characteristics, personalities, and abilities.

With such expertise, you may even re-evaluate the path to develop the needed skills for your triumph.

Do not start a pet shop if you are allergic to fur

Currently recruitment happens at striking speeds. Automation helps with the most *boring tasks*. One may think that entrepreneurs no longer need to know how to perform their core business activities, since it is so easy to hire, train and automate.

In other words, some people now think that individuals allergic to fur should run pet shops. People think that you could be always a remote entrepreneur, as long as you hire a *good manager*.

This belief ends with the sign of the first *agency problems* -

conflicts of interest inherent to relationships where one party act in another's interests. If you despise your core activity – or if it can kill you, like in the example of the allergic-to-fur entrepreneur – how to create the incentives necessary to avoid agency problems and motivate a *superb manager*?

How do you expect to select a good manager to perform a task you scorn? Even if you are not turning the dough yourself in your pancake restaurant, you still must be able to test your own product.

In this matter, if I could give only one counsel, would be this: even if the opportunity looks great, even if you see immense suppressed demand, do not start a company in a market you loathe. Be fond of your core business and try your core product. This is the way to excellency.

CHAPTER 11 – HOW TO MAKE A NEW BUSINESS ATTRACTIVE TO TALENTS?

It is not about the fridge full of ice cream.

During my last semester at the University of Sao Paulo, there was a book causing a corridor buzz. It was *Thinking, Fast and Slow*, by Daniel Kahneman, which covers, among other themes, human cognitive biases.

One of those cognitive biases is *loss aversion*. It means that a person losing $50 will be more unpleased than would be pleased by gaining $50.

This notion comes to my mind when I see startups still far from making their first profitable trimester investing in very expensive rewards to lure new employees. Things like unlimited holidays[27] or top-tier gym-memberships.

If their CEOs grabbed the concepts of cognitive biases, they would realize that expensive free perks:

> 1. Lose their motivating power across time, since people take it for granted.

2. Are easily replicable. If a competitor wants to *steal* your talented staff, they can just copy your policy of sending interns for "conventions" in 5-star hotels.
3. When the company faces adversities and needs to cut costs, removing the rewards will be more destructive than it was constructive to implement it in the first place.

This third point we can attribute to loss aversion. It is what happened when Upload, a virtual-reality company from Los Angeles, needed to cut one unusual (and expensive) perk. They had a tap free-flowing Kombucha - an expensive fermented tea from Manchuria, trendy in the Silicon Valley. As their founder, Taylor Freedman, explained in an interview to CNBC: *People would drink five glasses a day. It was $3,000 to $4,000 a month to have Kombucha on tap, so we had to shut it down. It was a big hit to the morale of the community.*

Avoid a similar situation by taking into consideration the 3 points above and answering: *Can we pay for this benefit even in a crisis?*

To conclude, it is good to notice that some benefits are costly, but they do pay for themselves and relate to the firm's core business. An example is the financial incentive Airbnb gives to employees to travel and stays in, well, *Airbnbs.*

Once decided which benefits you are offering (or not) to prospective employees, the next step is to pick what you are going to talk about during the interview.

Socio-cultural adaptations for Interviewing

Interviews do not happen in the same way everywhere. Do you remember the studies, mentioned in chapter 2, from Geert Hofstede? His indicators help to outline expectations to and of candidates.

Societies with high long-term orientation present candidates that would like to understand the career and development opportunities, while low-term orientation prospects will favor bonuses and short-term remuneration. The same is valid for other Hofstede factors like *Uncertainty avoidance*, where risk-taking societies like the US have candidates more fond of variable wages, while risk-averse cultures prefer a stable income.

The economic situation also plays a big role in how interviews happen. When I was living in South America, in a country with a two-digit unemployment rate, even qualified candidates had a firm stance of promoting their qualities to win the job. It made it easier for interviewers to know about previous experiences and achievements of candidates.

On the other side, when I arrived in Warsaw, the unemployment rate was below 3%, one of the lowest in Europe. I needed to build my team. With so many other jobs available everywhere, the interviews turned into me promoting the job opportunity for the candidates. This is not a problem *per se*, since the skill to promote your business has ample applications, like future capital raises.

Hire on time. Hire realistically.

According to Forbes Magazine, two of the biggest money-wasters for new companies are over-hiring and early hiring. The first means employing more brains and hands than you need for the early stages of a project. The second means contracting too soon.

Both problems deriving from overly optimistic planning and non-existence of buffers - time-reliefs to accommodate delays or below-expected business performance.

Hiring too early not only will waste money (since you are paying for a person who will not even have a desk), but also makes your business look unprepared and amateurish for the eyes of a recently built team.

Over-hiring is even worse. Having more people than you need means less work divided into more brains, what under-utilizes talent capacity and makes your entire business run in slow-march. The way to solve it - I think you guess it - is to let people go, but this can damage the group morale and create a crisis atmosphere.

Bottom line: do not hire people for your team based on your goals, but based on your most likely scenario.

Hire Slow, Recognize Fast

Another mistake I made – you may ask how I did not go bankrupt after so many mistakes – was to hire in a hurry.

Entrepreneurs know this is not wise. Still, one day either you will have excessive demand, or some of your employees will leave unexpectedly. When this happens, you enter the *hiring rush* and interview a few candidates. Even none of them matching your company profile (or your company matching their aspirations), you decide to employ one.

Few weeks after doing this mistake, one of the best from my team gave me a bold signal that I messed up. She just asked: *Levi, where do you find this kind of people?*. She did not mean it in a good way.

Take special care when you already have a committed and fine-tuned group. To put in your team a new member that does not match the spirit of the rest can be poisonous. I am not talking about distinct personalities here, but about different levels of commitment.

Once you find a candidate matching the quality of your team, recognize him fast. During the first weeks, he will seek to understand what is right and what is wrong, and positive reinforcement is crucial to guide your new member and speed up his performance.

Render to Caesar the things that are Caesar's. Have Skin in the Game

It is easy to start a fiery discussion regarding the positive or negative impacts of coffee on the human body. Debaters will find several scientific articles and researches to attack or defend caffeine. A similar phenomenon happens when the discussion is about remuneration.

One of the best books I read was *Freedom from Command and Control: Rethinking Management for Lean Service,* from John Seddon. The author makes a very solid case for fixed remuneration.

Contrarily, Silicon Valley startups normally have strong

policies of variable remuneration or equity bonus for employees.

How to decide the most appropriate method for remuneration? Nassim Taleb (mentioned already eight times in this book) answered this in his *Incerto* series: **skin in the game.**

There are situations where equity bonuses instead of fixed remuneration have dubious efficacy. A junior manager, in a corporation with thousands of employees, unlikely will see his higher efforts increase the company shares. There is no incentive, in this case, to seek a superb performance, because there is no benefit for his pockets. (Obviously, I am using a simplistic scenario, with no other potential incentives like promotions).

In new and smaller companies, the work of every single member has a visible impact. An extraordinary performance of a single team can reflect in the company result. Here, it makes all sense to go for equity or result remuneration.

Not always is possible to offer equity to your first employees. In my case, it was not viable, since the paperwork for it would be too expensive. But it is possible to offer a remuneration package with more *skin in the game* for every team member, where everyone earns more if the results are good. Quoting a famous Brazilian movie, *who wants to laugh, must first make others laugh*[28].

The Market Rate Dilemma

Probably you already saw more job ads offering *market-rate* salaries. I do not see how it makes sense since you are paying the same rate for people with performance above the market average (making them underpaid) and below-average (turning them overpaid).

If your product is solid and captivating, you should have no problem convincing candidates to accept equity or result remuneration as a wage component, instead of a full fixed *market rate* salary. If your prospective employees do not believe in your business proposition, either you are not selling your idea properly, or worse: your product is not that convincing.

It is easier to keep the team's good morale during a crisis if we also share the jackpot of a good season.

Hire Local.

In previous pages, I wrote about how well-funded startups waste money in unproductive ways. Ways that do not pay off and can be detrimental to business. One of them is the practice of hiring stars from rival companies to solve market problems to which your local staff cannot find a solution.

Jonathan Moisan, from AdvertisePurple, summarized in the following way[29]: *A lot of young startups think the help of someone who already knows everything and can come in elevating your company's market position is key. [...] If there is a person who already knows what your startup should do, why didn't they already solve the problem your company aims to solve?*

There are other reasons to think that recruiting high-performing staff from competitors can be a risky delusion. It is expensive if you need to match their current salary, and may create enemies inside your industry.

The company culture cocktail

When I was still an intern at a brokerage house during university, one of the senior brokers invited me to the after-office happy hour and offered me a gin tonic. I was not a fan of gin neither tonic water, so I was sure it would not be for my taste. But I found it great. When I told him about this strange effect of two things I disliked combining into a palatable taste, he told me that *gin tonic is a classic case of where the whole is greater than the sum of its parts, since they annul the bad notes and keep the good.*

As said before, an advantage every entrepreneur abroad should take benefit is to adopt best practices from his home country that, after proper testing, are suitable to his new environment. But when you are working with a team instead of alone, this requires extra care. In the same way a businessman needs time and effort to adapt, your team will need time and **resources** to understand and *buy* your ideas.

What are those resources? By far, the most significant is a good sales pitch from the founder to *sell* to his team why he is adopting certain foreign practices.

At this point, let me assure you one belief I held firm: *your team will never perform at their best if they just obey, but do not fully understand your foreign methods.* Be aware that I wrote *to understand*, not agree. While a unanimous agreement is great, it is not always achievable, but understanding should be reachable - if it is not, either the idea is not clear to yourself, or you should explain again, and better.

Am I telling you to spend time elucidation concepts and cultural insights brought from your origins?

Definitely I am. It is praiseworthy to make every member of

your team aware of best practices, and instead of being at odds, work in sync with your mission.

At the point where the team fully understands your imported best practices, and you fully understand the staff cultural norms (which are the local norms, if you followed my advice to hire local), you have both ingredients to do the *company culture cocktail.* Just like the tonic gin, the cultural knowledge brought by local employees will sum with your innovative best practices. All will turn into the entrepreneurial version of a refreshing gin tonic.

CHAPTER 12 – BENCHMARK, BENCHMARK, AND BENCHMARK. AFTER IT, REFINE YOUR GOALS.

All Good to Great companies began the process of finding a path to greatness by confronting the brutal facts about the reality of their business. When you start with an honest and diligent effort to determine the truth of your situation, the right decisions often become self-evident."

Jim Collins

Imagine you are driving a fast car in the *Autobahn 9*, the road connecting the German capital to Munich. Parallel to the highway, you slowly see a train approaching. The aerodynamic shape of the locomotive and continuous red stripe through the wagons reveals that this is the ICE *Schnellfahrt*, or simply ICE S, one of the fastest trains of Europe.

You get puzzled. The way the twenty thousand horsepower machine slowly approaches and overtakes your car raises the question: *why it is so slow, in such a straight and empty rail? Is it broken? Are those passengers from Berlin to Munich not in a hurry?*

After a moment of reflection, seeing the formidable train gently opens distance to you, you glance at the car velocimeter: 250km/h.

That is when you realize that the rail convoy was in reality dashing at three hundred kilometers per hour. Wrong benchmarking caused the illusion of the slow train.

How to know when your business is doing well, and when it is wrecking?

The first and most common answer would be "If we are having a profit, it is fine". It is a simplistic and often naïve attitude of new companies. If your profit is below the cost of capital or because of investments delayed, better postpone the celebrations.

Likewise, losses and negative margins are not synonymous with poor management or miscarried business. It may be just seasonality, local economic conditions, or, as during 2020, a global virus outbreak.

The high-speed train in our previous example looked slow because of how the human mind perceives relative speed. To see how fast it was would be enough to have a fixed point of reference. A benchmark – the point of reference for business – will help to avoid illusions in your entrepreneurial journey.

Benchmarking will give you peace of mind

Any hotel operator in a coastal city would be euphoric with lucrative summers and depressed during unprofitable winters if they did not benchmark. Managers of ski-resorts, on the other side, would have the opposite behavior.

This is not smart nor healthy, and it can get worse.

Do you remember the fable *The Ant and the Grasshopper*? If an entrepreneur gets deluded that he is doing very well without realizing that the success is just cyclical, he may not save for the winter, just like the grasshopper.

My favorite philosophical school is stoicism, and one of its teachings is that just a fool gets upset for not succeeding in something out of his control[30]. Therefore, that your business needed to navigate during the storms of a pandemic, a natural catastrophe or a social turmoil, it is not your fault. You could not avoid those things.

What you can do is to take action, control costs, and keep revenue streams alive during hard times. The only way to assess if you are doing it properly is to benchmark exhaustively. Benchmarking will show what to consider "normal".

Not always you will be able to benchmark. Sometimes you are the sole player in the region or in the whole industry. If your product is completely innovative, it's tricky to make comparisons with businesses that are similar but not the same. However, when you have an established pool of competitors, to compare indicators will draw the line in the sand.

Compare quality standards, costs, prices, and any indicator important to your core. But keep your soul.

You got how important is performance comparison when

venturing in unknown seas. But compare what? Which indicators you should benchmark against the competition?

Most conventional markets have their pre-established sets of indicators. A simple internet search for *performance indicators for + [business type]* will tell you beforehand what you need to measure against. Hint: get ready to see a bunch of acronyms.

Example of performance indicators:

Consulting firms: RPC (Revenue per client), CRR (Client Retention Rate), Repeat business rate, etc.

Restaurants: RevPASH (Revenue per Available Seat Hour), Food and beverage sales per guest, etc.

Hotels: RevPAR (Revenue per Room), Occupancy Rates, ADR (Average Daily Rate), etc.

Mobile App Company: CAC (Customer Acquisition Costs), Average Revenue Per User, Conversion Rate.

When implementing benchmark tools - often an electronic spreadsheet does the job well – remember to be aware of your firm specificities. Makes little sense for a low-cost airline to compare their average price to a first-class charter, since they make money in different ways - the low-cost carrier profit from selling things like extra luggage, while the first-class charter earns with all-included pricey tickets.

Remember that opportunities are not missed, but taken by someone else. Do you want to react quicker, discover tendencies, and grab prospects before everyone? Discover first how fast your car (or business) is against the train of the competition. Benchmark.

FINAL WORDS

To exchange the stability of a 9 to 5 job and the certitude of a monthly salary for the risks and challenges of entrepreneurship is a bold decision.

To be an entrepreneur far from home adds an entire magnitude to the challenges one must face. Together with the perils of any business, you have the additional complications of the language, cultural obstacles, and different laws. At the same time, people you always knew and could help are far, far away.

Do not see these challenges as deterrents, but ingredients to a great story, a priceless journey.

An entrepreneur I met in Brazil thought the same. He was a man that left his home in the northern region, around 80 years ago. In a time when nature floggings and drought scourges unleashed indiscriminate suffering, most residents turned into wretches and looked for safety in coastal areas.

But not this man. He turned his eyes much farther.

Taking nothing but his clothes and accompanied by no one but his wife, he endured days on the back of a truck, making a journey as long as the distance from Russia to Rome. His abilities were short, but his will was more than enough. He opened his business, starting an entrepreneurial tradition followed by many of his eight children and inspiring his grandson, which now thanks you for reading his book, and wishes you the best in your endeavor.

Improvise, adapt, overcome - in other words, if it doesn't work, think up a new plan. It is the key to survival.

Bear Grylls

APPENDIX - APPS AND TOOLS FOR THE ENTREPRENEUR ABROAD

To find a place to live: Some expats try to choose a place to live before arriving in their new country. To sign any contract based on pictures or videos can be unnecessarily risky and lead to disappointment. The best way to solve this problem is to rent a stress-free accommodation on a website like Airbnb while in your first weeks you visit your selected properties and choose properly. The advantage of Airbnb over other accommodation websites like Booking.com and Expedia is that frequently there are discounts for stays longer than a week.

To try it, download Airbnb by this link and win a $36 discount (or equivalent) in your first reservation. https://www.airbnb.com/c/jonataslevib?currency=USD

To learn the language and the culture: Some people are used to language apps like Duolingo. I am passionate about Lingq because of its extremely friendly interface, the community of users where everyone helps each other correcting exercises, the possibility of import books, articles, and songs to the app. You can use it to learn a new idiom and immerse in its culture at the same time. Using it I reached a conversational level in one of the hardest European languages, Polish, without going to any formal course.

You can check Lingq by visiting: http://bit.ly/36qzd6n

To transfer money between your old and new country: This recommendation saved me once, when just after arrival I realized I miscalculated the amount of money to bring. To do a normal international transfer would mean losing with poor exchange rates. Transferwise has rates much better than most banks, and their transfers may take less than 24 hours.

Create your account using this link and win $20 in your first transfer: http://bit.ly/2TVU0vZ

To not confuse currencies or overspend: XE currency converter is both a website and a mobile app easy to use and updated in real-time. Available at: https://www.xe.com/currencyconverter/

To compare the cost of living: There are two websites, each with millions of prices in their databases, which are essential to estimate if your salary will be enough to make the ends meet. They are Numbeo (https://www.numbeo.com/) and Expatistan (https://www.expatistan.com/)

To rent your former house or apartment and make some extra: I already recommended Airbnb before, but this time is for a different purpose. When we move out not completely sure if we will come back, or have no time to find a tenant or sell our property, a good solution can be to make it available at Airbnb for short-term rental. They even have tools to manage the property remotely and handle things like cleaning and insurance. It is not rare people making twice the amount of cash on Airbnb compared to what they would earn if they simply rented it for a single tenant.

You can check the option of becoming an Airbnb Host through this link (where you will also earn $10): http://bit.ly/36mBNKB

To have updates about the most cutting-edge tips and tricks for expats and long-term travelers: The blog of my consultancy firm, where I share weekly insights of life overseas. https://expatriateconsultancy.com/digital-nomads-expats-and-travellers-blog/

and my Facebook page: http://www.facebook.com/leviporai

DID YOU ENJOY THIS BOOK?

The greatest award I could have is your opinion. It would be wonderful to read your thoughts in Goodreads or Amazon.

Also, if you have friends or family moving out, remember how much you can help them by recommending this book.

Last but not least, we can keep in contact through my page: Levi Borba - Digital Nomad & Expat mentoring https://www.facebook.com/leviporai/or via my Medium page: https://leviborba.medium.com/

FROM THE SAME AUTHOR

Moving Out, Working Abroad and Keeping Your Sanity: 11 secrets to make your expat life better than you imagine

- **The most decisive expert for your success abroad and how to have free access to him.**

- The advice for your family you will never regret following. Neither they will.

- How to adapt to the local behaviors and etiquette in a matter of days.

- How to thrive like a native without being one.

Buy it in Amazon, here: https://www.amazon.com/dp/B084GF14CZ

Budget Travelers, Digital Nomads & Expats: The Ultimate Guide: 50 Tips, Tricks, Hacks and Ways.

Can you travel to 51 countries, in *every* continent, spending less than a used car?

- **The common opportunity when airlines charge almost 70% less for a flight (but still nobody uses it, except their employees).**
- How to pay less when renting an Airbnb.
- The perfect (and cheapest) time to look for housing or accommodation.
- **How to make airlines pay a 5-star hotel for you. With Breakfast included!**
- And other 43 hacks to make your travels inexpensive. Travel unlimited. And make every dollar count

Buy it in Amazon, here: https://www.amazon.com/

dp/B0886KVVMK

---

[1] You can check the complete ranking in https://www.heritage.org/index/ranking

[2] First publication in 1980, with a new edition in 2003 by Sage Pulications, *Culture's Consequences: Comparing Values, Behaviors, Institutions and Organizations Across Nations*; Hofstede, Geert.

[3] You can check each of those dimensions, as well simulate comparisons between different countries, at the website of *Hofstede Insights*: https://www.hofstede-insights.com/country-comparison/

[4] *4 reasons why a business plan is important*, iAfrikan, 2016. https://www.iafrikan.com/2016/06/15/4-reasons-why-a-business-plan-is-important/

[5] About this quote of Dwight D. Eisenhower: https://quoteinvestigator.com/2017/11/18/planning/

[6] The Civil War" by Caesar, translated with an introduction by Jane F. Gardner; Penguin Classics, London

[7] Raihani NJ and Bshary R (2015) Why humans might help strangers. *Frontiers in Behavioral Neuroscience.* Available at https://www.frontiersin.org/articles/10.3389/fnbeh.2015.00039/full

[8] Dixon, Rashan, *3 Steps to a Successful International Expansion,* Entrepreneur Europe, 2020. Available at https://www.entrepreneur.com/article/347047

[9] Definition from the Investopedia, available in: https://www.investopedia.com/terms/s/synergy.asp#:~:text=Synergy%20is%20the%20concept%20that,mergers%20and%20acquisitions%20(M%26A).

[10] Day, George; *Strategies for Surviving a Shakeout;* Harvard Business Review, March–April 1997 Issue. Available at: https://hbr.org/1997/03/strategies-for-surviving-a-shakeout

[11] Guttman, A; *Social media marketing penetration in the U.S. 2013-2019,* May 13, 2019

[12] Dahl, Darren; *10 Tips on How to Research Your Competition*; Inc.com. Available at https://www.inc.com/guides/201105/10-tips-on-how-to-research-your-competition.html

[13] 1 Corinthians 2:9 "*What no eye has seen, nor ear heard, nor the heart of man conceived, what God has prepared for those who love him*" Revised Standard Version Catholic Edition

[14] Mangel, M & Samaniego, F.J; *Abraham Wald's Work on Aircraft Survivability*; Journal of the American Statistical Association Vol. 79, No. 386 (Jun., 1984)

[15] Inglis-Arkell, Esther (May 2, 2013). "The frozen calm of normalcy bias". Gizmodo. Retrieved 23 May 2017.

[16] *Take 5: How to Adapt to Changes in Your Industry*, Kellogg Insight, Nov. 2017.

[17] Abrashoff, D. Michael. 2002. It's your ship: management techniques from the best damn ship in the navy. New York, NY: Warner Books.

[18] A *Buy and hold* investor is the one that buys stocks (or other securities as ETFs) and holds them for a long period, not taking decisions based on daily fluctuations. Meanwhile, a *day trader* or *swing trader* holds the securities for short time frames.

[19] You can check the full letter here: https://www.berkshirehathaway.com/letters/1986.html

[20] "Best Global Brands – 2014 (Interbrand) – Ranking The Brands". Rankingthebrands.com.

[21] Dixon, Rashan; *3 Steps to a Successful International Expansion*; March of 2020, Entrepreneur Europe. Available at https://www.entrepreneur.com/article/347047

[22] Complete quote available at https://www.goodreads.com/quotes/29138-be-like-water-making-its-way-through-cracks-do-not

[23] *Levantine* refers to the Levant, a region comprising Lebanon, Israel, Syria and surroundings.

[24] The 1932 Constitutionalist Revolution.

[25] Other travel hacks like this one you can find on one of my books, the Amazon best-seller in its category *Budget Travelers, Digital Nomads & Expats: The Ultimate Guide*.

[26] Numbeo and Expatistan are two online sources for price comparison between thousands of cities in the world. The first is available at https://www.numbeo.com/cost-of-living/ and the second at https://www.expatistan.com/cost-of-living.

[27] To see this and some unusual perks offered by tech companies, check the article *12 tech companies that offer their employees the coolest perks*, published TheNextWeb.com.

[28] The movie is *Elite Squad* ("Tropa de Elite" in the original version), from 2007.

[29] *14 Unnecessary Startup Expenses Wasting Hard-Earned Money*, Forbes Finance Council, Expert Panel, December of 2019.

[30] On the subject of being upset by changes out of control, I recommend the classical manuscript *Enchiridion*, from the greek philosopher Epictetus.

[L.1]acceptable

[L.2]indicate, claim

[L.3]the mindset makes it more likely to surrender

BOOKS BY THIS AUTHOR

Moving Out, Working Abroad And Keeping Your Sanity

Those methods helped HUNDREDS of foreigners across the globe.

The book recognized as the greatest step for a delightful life overseas (see reviews below).

Striking success as an expatriate, digital nomad or long-term traveller is only a few clicks away.

Budget Travelers, Digital Nomads & Expats: The Ultimate Guide

What I learned in my career as an airline specialist and hospitality entrepreneur allowed me to travel for a fraction of the normal prices.

Simple methods that if normal people used, they could travel the world still in their youth. Methods that allowed me to travel to 51 countries spending less than a used car. Methods for YOU to travel with comfort and Hyper-Low budget. Only few dollars separate you from the life you should live.

In those pages, there are secrets like:

The frequent opportunity when airlines charge near 70% less for a flight (but still nobody uses it, except their employees).

How to pay less when renting an Airbnb.

The hack to not pay for excess luggage. NEVER.

The perfect time to look for housing or accommodation and save money.

The one single phrase to say to a Hotel receptionist that make you upgraded.

How to visit places like the Greek Islands, Cyprus, Malta or Sicily paying almost 67% less.

How to make airlines pay a 5-star hotel for you. With breakfast included!